Praise

Travis Garrison's book ... players, parents and coaches to understand ... ... someone who has fought through many difficult obstacles at every level of his basketball career both on the court and off. This book is a learning tool for all ages.

Coach Morgan Wootten
Retired Head Basketball Coach
DeMatha Catholic High School
Member of Basketball Hall of Fame

Never Satisfied is a blueprint for today's generation of athletes of how to manage the triumphs and pitfalls that the business of basketball throws their way. We all are chasing our dreams and in this book, Travis gives players, parents, and coaches a roadmap to reach those dreams.

Mike Jones
Head Basketball Coach
DeMatha Catholic High School

Travis Garrison is a remarkable man both on and off the court. He has played at every level and has experienced the good, the bad, and the ugly that basketball offers. Never Satisfied gives tremendous insight into all of his experiences and is a must read for players, coaches, and parents. His message is invaluable.

Alan Stein
Strength & Conditioning Coach
Owner of Stronger Team

I have watched Travis grow in the person that he is today since middle school. He has been successful at every level of basketball and his book gives you the blueprint as to how he did it. Follow it and the sky is the limit!

Lamar Butler
George Mason University
Point Guard 2006 Final Four Team

Every athlete knows that the road to success and victory is not easy. There are hardships, obstacles, battles, and continual difficulties along the way that must be faced, and most are faced alone. I know this because as a former professional athlete and also a former student athlete, I faced many of these things on my own road. But now Travis Garrison has given not only athletes, young and old, a manual for some of the things we face and how we can deal with them he has also given their families, friends, and coaches a look inside the world of athletes and how they can help them overcome these challenges. Never Satisfied: An Athletes Battle *will give each of you who read it a look the complex and arduous journey of an athlete who may or may not get to his ultimate goal, but will always fight til the end to come out on top. It will also equip young athletes and the people who love them with the tools and wisdom they will need as they prepare to take this journey and hopefully not only win on the court, but also in the biggest game of them all, the game of life. You will soon learn, after every victory there is another mountain to climb which is why most of us are never satisfied!*

Laron Profit
University of Maryland
Former NBA Player
Washington Wizards & LA Lakers

Travis has written a book that is a must read for any player, parent or coach. The reader has the ability to learn from all the things he has experienced. Here is a guy who has always played basketball at the highest level. Travis has been where they want to be.

Neal Murphy
Assistant Basketball Coach
DeMatha High School 1985-2007

I have known Travis Garrison his whole basketball life. He is like a little brother to me. I've trained him, had many heart to heart talks and given him advice after his successes and failures. It's been an amazing journey. Basketball is what he does to earn a living but who he is you'll find out after as you read the story of his life and LOVE HIM UNCONDITIONALLY as I do!

Keith "The Shot Doc" Veney

Travis and I became brothers during our time at DeMatha together and this hold true to this day. With all of his successes, seeing him as the best husband and father he could possibly be, is his greatest accomplishment in my eyes.
          Elijah Brooks
          Head Football Coach
          DeMatha Catholic High School
          & Former High School Teammate

Travis and I have known one another for a long time, I dont consider him a friend, I consider him a brother. He and I have similar stories and often times rely on one another for support during difficult times. Travis has matured into a great man, he is a hard worker, he is spiritual, family oriented, intelligent and honest. He is only scracthing the surface with this book, there is so much more we can expect from him and he is someone I am extremely proud of. I'm honored to have met Travis and encourage young people to learn from him as he is a good example of what hardwork and determination can get you.
          Alpha Bangura,
          St. John's University
          & Libyan National Team

Never Satisfied

Sudden Change Media
Washington, DC

Never Satisfied

An Athlete's Battle

The Successes and Self-Doubts of
a Baller on the Way to Manhood

TRAVIS GARRISON

Never Satisfied: *An Athlete's Battle*
Copyright © 2012 by Travis Garrison

ISBN-13 978-0615687407
ISBN-10 0615687407

All rights reserved. No part of this publication may be reproduced, stored in a retrieval system, or transmitted in any form or by any means – electronic, mechanical, photocopy, recording, or any other –except for brief quotations in printed reviews, without the prior written permission from the publisher.

Additional copies of this book can be purchased at:

www.neversatisfiedtg.info

Contact Travis Garrison at:

tgneversatisfied@gmail.com

www.facebook.com/tgneversatisfied

Twitter: @Garrisonhoops

Address requests for information to:

Sudden Change Media
455 Massachusetts Avenue, NW #150-144
Washington, DC 20001

publisher@suddenchangemedia.com

Dedication

This book is dedicated to ALL of my family and friends, those who stuck by me through not only the good times but the bad as well. You all have always supported my dreams, and gave me encouragement when I needed it the most. If it wasn't for you, I do not know where I would be today. So I thank you and I love you.

A special dedication goes to Gabriel Kalaw, the young man who inspired and encouraged me to write this book. If it wasn't for you, I wouldn't have had the courage to share my story. Thank you!

About the Author

Travis Garrison grew up in Suitland, Maryland with his mother and two older brothers. He was a star at DeMatha Catholic High School where he played for the legendary Hall of Fame coach Morgan Wootten. His individual honors included being a McDonald's All-American, a Michael Jordan All-Star, and a Washington Post All-Met player. He graduated from DeMatha in June 2002.

Coach Gary Williams recruited Travis to play for his defending National Champion Maryland Terrapins. He was part of a highly touted recruiting class that led Maryland to its first ACC title in twenty years. Travis was a three-year starter and his up and down career at Maryland are an important part of why he has written this book, *Never Satisfied: An Athlete's Battle*.

After some post-draft workouts for NBA teams and the NBA D-League, Travis was Rookie of the Year in the CBA playing for the Great Falls Explorers in Montana. In addition to playing in North America, his basketball skills have taken him to teams in South America, Asia, Europe, and Eastern Europe.

Off the court, Travis is passionate about helping others, especially young players. He speaks at basketball camps and plans to be working with youth full-time after his professional basketball career is over.

Travis returns to his home in Washington, DC in the spring and summer off season to be with his wife, Vanessa, and their children Jonas and TJ. They are expecting their third child.

Table of Contents

Acknowledgments xv

Foreword by Coach Mike Jones xvii

Introduction 19

1   Where it All Started: Family 21

2   Loving the Game: Youth Basketball 35

3   Learning from a Legend: DeMatha Basketball 43

4   Travis Garrison: McDonald's All American 55

5   Swagger and Self-Doubt: Maryland Basketball 65

6   Losing it All: Bad Decisions 77

7   Starting Over: NBA Dreams 85

8   Reputation and Consequences:
     The CBA and Around the World 95

9   More than Just a Baller: Becoming a Man 113

The Million Dollar Question 119

Acknowledgments

I am indebted first to my wife Vanessa, my companion, friend, lover and supporter. She keeps me grounded and has lifted me up whenever I get discouraged. Our children, TJ and Jonas, and even our unborn daughter Madelyn, bring joy to my life every day. Daddy loves you.

I also wish to thank my mother, Sheila, for providing a home where we were loved unconditionally. She taught us how to be men of God, and the true value of life. I could not have done it without you, Mom!

My two brothers, Lawrence and Shavery, have played a critical role in my life by their example of hard work and always being there for me. They taught me about the game of basketball and life, and taught me to never give up, and always work hard.

I am blessed to have the support of my father, who taught me how to work for everything, and that nothing is ever given, but earned. I was blessed further by also having several father figures in my life who taught me many life lessons, especially my Godfather Lawrence Goodwin. Many of the lessons you taught me are still with me to this day. Thank you.

Coaches are very special people. Most do not get paid nearly enough for all of the time that they put into helping other people's children. I am only able to name a few here, but I am grateful for the contribution that each coach has made to my life as a basketball player and as a person.

Special thanks must go to my coaches at DeMatha High School beginning with Coach Wootten. He is still like a father to me. He is one of the main reasons I am still playing basketball. He was not only a coach, but a mentor and teacher who challenged us as not only as players, but also as people. Also, assistant coach Neal Murphy who let me know the things I needed to do on and off the court, especially when I wasn't doing right in school. He would always give it to me like it was, always honest with me. And finally, coach Mike Jones who was an assistant when I was at DeMatha and is now DeMatha's head coach. Coach Jones was another person who showed me how to work hard, and push myself to the limit. He was not only telling us what to do but he was on the court working out with us; so he was leading by example.

He was kind enough to agree to write the foreword to this book. He always shoots straight with his players and parents and, like Coach Wootten and Coach Murphy, cared about my life on and off the court.

Difficult times may tend to define us more than the easy times. Coach Gary Williams was the right coach for me when I was going through so much at the University of Maryland. His intensity and honesty are still something I aspire to in my life.

Finally, thanks to Coach Curt Ashburn, my editor and publisher at Sudden Change Media who put so much time and energy into helping my dream and passion come to life. He had the same enthusiasm to do this book as I did, and helped to make my dream a reality. So thank you Coach Ashburn for all of your hard work and dedication.

Foreword

As the Head Coach at DeMatha Catholic High School, I am fortunate to work with some tremendous young men. I am proud of them all. Whether it be the NBA, corporate America, or the normal everyday nine to five, our guys are first rate men and good members of the community. That certainly applies to Travis Garrison.

I was first introduced as an Assistant Coach on Morgan Wootten's staff at DeMatha Catholic High School at the Metropolitan Area Basketball School in July of 1998. When I was introduced to the current DeMatha players, there was one who stood out to me immediately. I recognized his face, but it was a lot older than I had remembered. The fourteen year olds name was Travis Garrison. I had grown up playing against his older brother Lawrence who you will read about in the book. I had seen Travis when he was much younger, big smile, firm handshake, and already six feet five inches or taller. Potential? YES, without a doubt.

It seemed as though I knew Travis already. Pretty soon, I would get to know him even better. I had just finished a four-year professional career that had taken me all over the world. An injury and pressure from family had me ready to move on to the "real world" to get a "real job." I had always wanted to be a coach and the opportunity to work for and with the soon-to-be Hall of Famer Morgan Wootten was the perfect place to start. I had always thought coaching was the next best thing to playing. Little did I know that the young man that I recognized that day would help my transition to coaching and also in becoming the coach I am today.

After spending some time with Travis, it was clear that he was a special young man. What also became evident is that he needed some balance. Many of his admirers spent all of their time telling him how great he was and how the NBA was a sure thing and he was a "can't miss" prospect. Through our conversations, it was evident that he just was a typical boy; one that, deep down, wanted to be told the truth and enjoyed time around people that didn't want something from him. He wanted to be normal!

I felt as though this was the role that I was to have for Travis and others that came after him. My time spent with him would not be solely based in his future as a basketball player, nor would it be filled with talk of the fame and fortune that everyone had promised him was sure to come.

My home in Upper Marlboro, Maryland took me down Pennsylvania Avenue twice each day. The Garrison Family home was just off Pennsylvania Avenue in Suitland. The drive from DeMatha in Hyattsville to Suitland can take anywhere from twenty-five to fifty minutes depending on traffic. After the off-season workouts in the fall and spring, I usually drove Travis home.

Unlike most teenagers, who would take advantage of that time to sleep, Travis and I would cover the full gamut, from school to girls to basketball to music to social issues. You name it, and we talked about it. It was during these times that Travis could speak freely and be himself. I really came to know him as a person. I knew what happened on his last recruiting visit or AAU trip, why his favorite teacher seemed to be on him more than the other students. Did he favor Nike or Adidas? Who was the best rapper alive? How was he going to take care of his mom and brothers one day?

The kid that always had a smile on his face and seemed to enjoy life would surprise me with "real" discussions about what happened in his neighborhood the previous night or what the latest college recruiter had promised him. We would argue about what song was the best on Jay-Z's "Blueprint" album and he wanted me to play JaRule and Ludacris over and over again.

The times were fun and made our relationship stronger. I would tell him of my brief career after college and all the things that he should do to ensure that he would go much further. I am so proud of Travis. This book allows him to give back. *Never Satisfied* is a blueprint for today's generation of athletes of how to manage the triumphs and pitfalls that the business of basketball throws their way. We all are chasing our dreams and in this book, Travis gives players, parents, and coaches a roadmap to reach those dreams. It is a must have and I am so proud of Travis for providing a true testimony so that others can learn from him.

Mike Jones
Head Basketball Coach
DeMatha Catholic High School

Coach Jones has taken the storied DeMatha basketball program to even higher levels of play with teams that are perenially ranked among the top-ten in the country.

Introduction

I have wanted to write this book for several years. Now that my life has settled down and I have a wife and family, I have been reflecting more on my basketball career and the path I've taken. I think that I have had enough success and made enough mistakes to have something to say to other young athletes who love the game of basketball as I do.

This book is written for players, parents, and coaches; but from my standpoint as a player. My children are still very young and I have never coached, so I do not pretend to be an expert on either subject. However, I do know the experiences I have had with my parents and coaches, and the impact they've had on my life and career.

In high school, I had a goal of attaining the honor of being named a McDonald's All-American. Looking back, I am proud of having achieved that goal, but that title also came with high expectations which, at the time, I welcomed. I was on top of the world when I graduated from DeMatha Catholic High School. I played for Coach Morgan Wootten, the best basketball coach ever. That was the opinion of the great John Wooden and it sure is mine as well.

Coach Wootten and his staff did all they could to prepare me for basketball and for life. But the other half of preparation is execution, and the next four years at the University of Maryland, and the six years since, have not turned out like they were "supposed to" for the "can't miss" kid from Suitland, Maryland.

A lot was expected of the recruiting class of 2002 for the Maryland Terps. Coach Gary Williams' team had won the National Championship the year before and I went there to carry on that tradition, leave school early, and go to the NBA. Here, in this book, I will discuss the factors that led to me not taking that route.

I have "Never Satisfied" tattooed on my arm because that's how I try to live my life. When I was younger, it was always about being a better basketball player; but now, as the title of my book implies, it is also about always striving to be a better man.

Someone told me that a good book has to be more than just an interesting story. There has to be a "so what" to make it special. The "Fouls and Free Throws" at the end of each chapter are the "so what" of my book and of my life. And just as an added bonus, later in the book, I answer the million-dollar question that people ask me all the time!

It is my hope that by sharing my story, I am able to help young athletes, families, and coaches, learn something from my successes and my failures, and use what I've been through to assist them along the way as they navigate the world of basketball.

1

Where It All Started

Family

Maryland Terrapins coach Gary Williams called me and said, "It's out." My heart sank. Earlier an assistant coach had grabbed me after my class and told me, "You have to turn yourself in to the police, Travis." I had gotten into an altercation with a woman in a bar, but that was three months ago, in October. This was Friday the thirteenth of January, 2006, and from this day forward, my life would be changed.

The Chief of Police of Hyattsville was a DeMatha alumnus, so I turned myself into him. He was discreet about it, but I was still devastated when I was handcuffed. I had seen criminals on TV shows being booked and fingerprinted, but now the ink was on my fingers and I could not believe this was happening.

"It's out," was an understatement. The headline on the front page of the Washington Post sports section the next morning said, in big letters, "Terrapins' Garrison is Charged with Assault and a Sex Offense." The reporter tried to contact me, but I was not taking calls, so the story ran with only my accuser's version and it showed me in the worst possible light.

They made sure to mention that I was six-foot eight-inches and 240 pounds. They mentioned that my teammate Chris McCray was a witness. I didn't want anyone else dragged into this, but the story had a life of its own. I had no one to blame but myself. I should not have been in that bar in the first place.

It was the lead story on ESPN all day that Saturday—Travis Garrison "slaps a woman." I was humiliated. The internet sports boards exploded with the story. It was everywhere. I went in to see Gary and he said that I would be suspended for one game, but that there would be no other punishment before the case went to court.

In reality, the punishment had already started and it haunts me to this day. It wasn't supposed to happen this way. Not to me, not to Travis Garrison, McDonald's All-American. But to really understand the lessons to be learned from the lowest point in my life, you need to know a little of how I got to the highest.

I am the youngest of three boys and grew up in a single parent household. The oldest is my brother Lawrence. He is older than me by nine years. My other brother, Shavery, is six years older than me. You can just imagine what it was like growing up with two brothers who are significantly older. They bossed me around and made me do things they themselves didn't want to do. I guess that's what little brothers are for. We lived in a small apartment in Oxon Hill, Maryland until I was about three years old and then we moved into a house in Suitland, Maryland. It was a nice neighborhood and much safer than where we had previously lived.

Many times, when you are the youngest sibling in your family, you tend to look up to the older brothers or sisters in your family. You try to be like them because you think that everything they do is cool. That was definitely true in my case. I was one of those kids that always wanted to fit in or be accepted. To be honest, and this is important, I'm still like that in a way.

My brothers always seemed to be in the spotlight, and I remember sometimes going to extreme measures for attention. Believe it or not, I was not one of those children who were really into sports. Until I was about eight-years old, I didn't really care too much for basketball or any other sports for that matter. Both of my brothers were playing basketball and I was the little kid at the games with G.I. Joes playing in the stands or running the halls.

When my brother Shavery was about thirteen and I was seven, I remember going to watch him play football at the local Boys and Girls Club field on Saturdays. I threw the football around at the field pretending to be a football player like him and begging my mom for some football equipment so I could feel like an actual football player.

I also remember trying to play catch with Shavery in front of our house and I couldn't catch the ball at all. He said I had no hands. I don't know how it came about, but probably because I wanted to wear the equipment so badly, that I joined the same football team as Shavery, but in the lower weight group.

I was considered the soft one compared to my brothers and I don't know what I was thinking, but playing football was a disaster! From what I remember, it was not good at all.

One time, I came face to face with a wide receiver who was heading right for the goal line and the only thing that stood between him and the end zone was me. Let's just say that was probably one of the easiest touchdowns he got all season.

One of my coaches gave me a nickname, "Cornbread." To this day I don't know why I was given that name, but I'm pretty sure it wasn't for a good reason. I think coaches need to be careful that something they think is funny doesn't negatively label a kid. After games, the members of my team would count the number of color marks they had on their helmets from the opposing team's helmets. Everyone else had a lot, but me, well, not too many.

My uniform would barely be dirty, so one game I decided to change that. I was going out there just to accomplish that goal, to get dirty. I think I got called with a late hit while trying to get my uniform dirty. To be honest, I was not really a fan of all the contact, but I guess I just wanted to be like Shavery. He is the more physical one out of the three of us, so that sport suited him more than it did me and he was also really good at it.

I stuck it out for the whole season and the following year I came back for two or three practices before I quit. I never regretted trying football. That was the only way to really find out if it was for me. I don't know if I thought about it then (probably not), but children should be encouraged, not forced to try different sports. Now at least I have a cool picture of myself in a football uniform!

My oldest brother Lawrence, we call him L or LG, was the brains out of the three of us. I remember him dragging me to his basketball games because my mom had three jobs and my brothers had to take me wherever they went. So L used to take me to his games.

I paid very little attention to what was going on in the games and mostly played with one of his teammate's brothers. We used to run and play in the halls and, when he wasn't at the games, I would look for someone else to play with. L was a hard worker and I couldn't help notice how much he put into getting better. He used to be at the court all day. I would see him jumping rope in the middle of the street and doing calf-raises on the steps in our house. He would do anything and everything you can think of to become a good basketball player. That continues to inspire me to this day.

I remember him watching Michael Jordan "Come Fly with Me" tapes before his games. Since I was stuck with my brothers growing up, or rather, they were stuck with me, I picked up some good habits from them. L used to take me to the court with him. He played against guys from different neighborhoods and there was a lot of battling going on. It was street ball and it was rough. After they played, he would stay after and shoot and still be there working out when the sun went down.

I recall one time like it was yesterday. He brought me on to the court and showed me the proper way to shoot the basketball. He showed me the right form and how to release the ball. That night stayed with me for a long time. Shavery also used to take me with him to the court; but I was much smaller than they were and they only let me play once in a while. When they let me play, they didn't take it easy on me. I had to work for everything and I didn't like that. So sometimes I just quit and walked off the court with Shavery yelling at me about having to work for the ball and my points. I didn't care; I was mad and just wanted to go home.

My brothers are a big reason that I like to help younger players. I got much tougher from going head to head with L and Shavery and the guys from the neighborhood. The fact that they did not take it easy on me made it rough at the time, but when I started playing against boys my own age, it seemed a lot easier.

I really didn't have too much in the way of skills; I just had a little height. Some of my friends were much better than me, mainly the older ones. I did not like that at all. I remember as I got older I continued to play with them and they still roughed me up and treated me like I was their age even though I was much younger.

Travis between his older brothers Shavery (l) and Lawrence (r)

When I was eight years old, I joined the District Heights Boys and Girls Club basketball team. This was another comical year for me in sports; I was the tallest kid on the team and had zero skills, just height. I didn't know what I was doing; I was pretty much just out there. To a basketball coach, I looked like a valuable asset because of my height. That may have been true, but I needed a lot of work.

Well, the season that I was eight is vague to me; but I do have one funny story about that season that I remember very clearly. Now remember how I told you that my oldest brother L used to watch Michael Jordan tapes before games? Well, I looked up to L, so I also wanted to watch them. I think that may have been a bad idea because you know Michael Jordan was doing a lot of high flying dunks.

I thought they were really cool and wanted to try them myself. I remember being in a game and after stealing the ball, I was all by myself on the break. Now mind you, I had just watched a Michael Jordan tape and the famous take off from the free throw line. As I was dribbling across half court, my adrenaline started getting more intense. As I got closer to the free throw line, I was seeing Michael do his dunk in my mind; so I thought hey, let me give it a try.

Here I was eight-years old and trying to dunk from the free throw line. Not surprisingly, my flight was pretty short. I took off and landed about one step inside the free throw line. All I could do was throw the ball hard off the backboard. I was subbed out of the game as fast as I came in. My coach asked me what I was doing. I said, "Trying to dunk". He shook his head and sat me down. That was one of my fondest memories from my first year playing basketball.

My coach tried to teach me something about the game and how to use my size. That was a great idea because I was much taller than other kids my age, but it still took me time to get the game down. By then I was actually working on my game when I played with my friends in the neighborhood. My older friends were good and competitive at every sport. I wasn't quite there yet, but they were pushing me to get better because of their desire to win.

When I was nine years of age I played ball for Bradbury Heights Boys and Girls Club. Being a year older, I was a little better at basketball, but still had a ways to go. My coach was a woman. She was a very good coach and really knew the game. She had a son that played on the team and he was really good. He actually made me better because we played the same position. The skills he possessed made me want to work more on my own skills.

I had a solid year that season. It is still kind of vague to me, but one thing I do remember is that my coach made me watch the Washington Bullets play and then I had to tell her Chris Webber's stats. I guess she wanted me to play like him.

I also remember we played a game against another team and she didn't think I was rebounding enough. After the game, she kept me behind and wanted me to imagine that she put a dollar on the top of the backboard. She told me to try to jump up there and get it. She said that's how I want you to jump for rebounds, like I put a dollar on top of the backboard and you were trying to get it. She was very nice and definitely helped me with my game.

She probably does not even remember that, but coaches have such a powerful impact on their players. I was very fortunate to have many fine coaches. It is obvious to everyone that Morgan Wootten and Gary Williams were outstanding coaches. I only hope that any youth league coaches who are reading this book realize how long lasting an impact they also have on their players.

What was good was that all of this competition was making me tougher. Remember earlier I said that I was considered the soft one in our family. The neighborhood games were really rough. There was definitely a lot of battling going on and I was getting tougher. I didn't walk off the court and quit anymore, but I still had a lot of work to do on my skills. I was learning a valuable lesson--don't quit and be honest with yourself and others.

I continued to watch L work hard. This guy was a workaholic. He would be in the middle of the street in front of our house jumping rope, dribbling the ball, whatever and whenever. It didn't matter what time of the day it was either. I remember him buying a pair of shoes; I believe they were called strength shoes. They looked like something from outer space and were supposed to make your calves stronger and help you jump higher. He walked around with those on up and down the street.

I also continued to go to the basketball court with Shavery. He and his friends still beat up on me. I had to earn everything I got on the court. I was smaller and younger, but looking back at those years I realize that all of those things got me to where I am today. When I got older, I never understood why people thought I was not tough enough. I grew up playing street ball and being physically tough was the only way to survive.

Throughout my basketball career I have been encouraged by a lot of people to be more aggressive. Eventually, the encouragement turned into criticism. I have been asked more times that I can count why I do not dunk with two hands or dunk a lot. I have never told anyone this story, but the purpose of this book is to help young players handle criticism, so here is the reason why I always dunk with one hand if I do choose to dunk.

When I was about nine years old, I was shooting baskets with my friend Jamar Short. We were at one of those eight-foot baskets and Jamar was dunking with ease, so I told Jamar to watch me dunk. I dribbled to the basket and imitated the two-handed slam-dunk that I had seen the pros do. As I went up and tried to slam the ball down hard with two hands, I suddenly felt myself falling backwards. I had hit the rim with the ball, got hung and was headed for the ground.

Instinctively, I caught myself on my right elbow and that kept the back of my head from getting cracked open. We both laughed, but inside I could not stop thinking what might have happened if I had not used my elbow to break my fall. It might not make sense to all my critics, but ever since then I have dunked with one hand. If you look at any shots of me dunking, you will see my off elbow trailing behind me. That is a subconscious response to a fear that was planted in me at nine years old.

I hope that players, parents, and coaches will learn from that story. Not dunking or dunking with two hands has nothing to do with not being tough or aggressive; it is a psychological barrier that I have never been able to overcome. The criticisms never did anything to help me, they only created self-doubt. The athlete's toughest battle is not against the other team or another player, it is the battle within that is the biggest challenge.

Being good and becoming great at anything takes hard work. I have had role models all of my life who passed their great work ethic on to me. As you know by now, my brother Lawrence had a deep influence on me. He was the one who told me, "While you aren't working out, the other guy is." But it wasn't until I sat down to write this book that I realized that it wasn't just L who taught me to work hard. Every person who was important to me when I was growing up contributed to my strong work ethic.

For instance, my mom worked hard to support our family. The reason I was always with my brothers is that my mom was working three jobs. Even after coming home from work, it didn't seem to matter how tired she was; if there was work to do, she kept going until it was done. Yard work, housecleaning, taking out the trash; her attitude was and still is that you do what you have to do to get the job done.

Working and going to church were her two main activities. She has always been the religious one in the family; but as far as basketball goes, she has no knowledge at all. She really had no interest in the sport; she only cared about basketball because her sons were always playing it. Even though she did not know enough to give me any coaching tips at any level, she was always there to cheer for me. Parents, take an interest in what your children are interested in doing. It means so much for a child to hear your voice from the stands, even if, like my mom, you have no idea what the heck is going on!

The big thing for my mom was my school work. She wanted me to go to the best schools possible. She worked hard and expected us to work hard in school. To be honest, I just wanted to play with my friends and, as I got older, I just wanted to ball. School was always something I had to do in order to be allowed to play basketball. What I did not realize when I was younger was that high school and college were a lot easier the harder you worked in elementary and middle school. Once I got to DeMatha it was too late to make up for lost time, so school was always harder than it had to be.

My dad is a pastor and he also valued hard work and demanded that I work hard, too. When I was with him, he made me work. There was always some project to do. His motto was, "Nothing is given to you; you have to work for it." There was no such thing as just getting up in the morning and having breakfast. Nope, I had to work for my breakfast!

As you can see, I was surrounded by hard working people. I didn't like it at the time, but those examples stayed with me. Whenever my game was in a slump, it was hard work and making sure I was still having fun that got me through. Talent can be in a slump, skills can be in a slump, but hard work and enjoying the game is never in a slump. If you can't out play them, out work them.

The disciplinarian in my life was not just my mom or my dad, but my Godfather, Lawrence Goodwin. Larry was an architect. Not surprisingly, everything had to be precise and done right with Larry. My mom really counted on him and my dad to take care of any discipline I needed. I am grateful to them for their high expectations. I think that is one reason why "never satisfied" became the theme of my life.

As grateful as I am for all of the people who helped shape my life in my younger years, it was my brother Lawrence who really raised me. He took me everywhere he went even when he didn't want to have his little brother hanging around. The thing I remember most is that he could play some ball and I respected him, and still do. He made me do things right and I modeled my basketball play after him. If there is one lesson that I could pass on to every player reading this book, it would be what he taught me about hard work, "Remember, Travis, while you are not working, the other guy is."

Another basketball influence in my life was my Uncle Daryel Garrison who played for Missouri State and wore jersey #32. He still holds several records there including the all-time scoring record. He was only the fourth player in school history to have his jersey retired. He got hurt before he was able to play with the Philadelphia 76ers. He was the one who really taught my brothers and me about the game.

My uncle Daryel is the one who taught my oldest brother how to shoot, which was then passed on to me. He loved to trash talk and to challenge us to play one-on- one. He was really battling with my brothers rather than with me because I was too young to really be any competition at the time. But just watching him play and seeing his moves made me realize which side of the family the basketball talent comes from.

When I visited Kansas as I got older, he would take me to the court and teach me a thing or two. One time really sticks out. On one of my visits when I was about eleven years old, we went to a recreational center in a rough neighborhood where there were a lot of kids playing. We played against them and they knew who my uncle was so I felt safe. As we played he pointed out the mistakes I made and kind of got on me. At one point, he just left while I was in the middle of a game. I was kind of nervous because I was there by myself and knew no one. But I knew what he was trying to do. He wanted to get me around a group of kids who were older and who would make me tougher. It worked; after a while, I felt comfortable and held my own.

Every time I went to Kansas I was more prepared than the time before. During one trip when I was about 16, I finally beat my uncle. He may have been a little older but still, I beat him. I felt as though that was a huge accomplishment, like beating the teacher. I still brag about it to this day! It really boosted my confidence as a player.

I also have an aunt named Angie who played ball and I was told that, if there was a WNBA back when she played, she would have been drafted. She was not shy when it came to critiquing my game and always gave me pointers. That made me work on my game more because I knew she knew what she was talking about.

So, in a sense, I come from a basketball family. I began this chapter at the low point of my life. The first thing I did when I left the police station that day was call my family. Family is everything. When you are younger you do not always appreciate the importance of family; but when life hits you with challenges, on and off the court, it's your family who will be there for you.

Even though my mother never knew much about the sport, when she found out that I was writing this book, she wanted to write a letter to all the readers. Parents, sometimes it might seem as if your children do not appreciate you but hang in there. Make sure your children know they can always come home, or like me, call home when their world has fallen apart.

Here is my mom's letter:

As a parent, I always wanted the best for Travis and his brothers. I never wanted to live my dreams through them, but wanted them to dream and succeed at whatever it was they wanted. One thing that I would always preach to them was to, "Put God first in your life and do your very best at whatever you do."

I watched Travis grow from this young kid who did not show much interest in sports to becoming a McDonald's All-American basketball player. He tried football but after getting knocked down by those defensive players, he gave up on football. I encouraged him through the good and bad times, letting him know that in life, there will be some disappointments, but to keep his head up. We also talked about mistakes you will make, but learn from them.

Some years ago, I was in Smithfield, North Carolina, and ran into a parent whose son played on a team with Travis when they were ten years old. We laughed and joked about how uncoordinated Travis was at that time and now he has turned out to be a great player. His practice and hard work really paid off. Travis—I love you son! I'm so proud of you for taking this opportunity to share with others your ups and downs as an athlete and how you had the courage not to give up.

Mom

FOULS AND FREE THROWS

Energy and excitement create a love of sports!

Parents: Allow your children to try different sports rather than forcing them into one that you want them to play. Sometimes I see kids that look miserable playing a sport, and you can tell they do not want to be there. Once, I saw a parent making his kid jump rope and train for hours. The kid looked no older than ten. You could just tell the kid was not happy and did not want to do it. I always believed that things you decide to do on your own will be more fun and will lead to more success.

When you have a choice, find coaches who allow the kids to enjoy the game. The younger the players, the more a coach should emphasize having fun. Understand, however, that winning is a lot more fun than losing, so coaches of young players need to be balanced. Constructive criticism is part of coaching, but good coaches do it in a way that the child will understand and is not traumatized.

Players: Enjoy the game! Try different sports, as many as you can. You never know which one you might fall in love with. I found that when I tried to play football, that it was NOT the game for me. I was simply playing the sport because my brother played. My mother wanted me to try different sports, like baseball. Out of fear, I told her I did not want to play because I was afraid that the ball would hit my hand. Looking back I wish I would have tried it. There's a lot of money to be made there!

Cameron Wake came to DeMatha a year ahead of me to play basketball, which was his first love. He was very good, but he gave football a try his junior year. He never had big-time success in basketball, but he went on to play football for Penn State University and then in the Canadian Football League before making it in the NFL. He just signed a 49-million-dollar contract with the Miami Dolphins. What if he had never tried football?

2

Loving the Game

Youth Basketball

By the time I was eleven years old, my skills were improving, but my overall knowledge of the game was still not very good. I finally figured out what an assist was and the only basketball I ever watched on television was when Michael Jordan was playing. Other kids were going to summer basketball camps, but I started playing some AAU ball and I was now self-motivated.

I no longer needed my brothers or a coach to motivate me. In the summer, I would get up and eat breakfast and run to the courts. I was in the sun so much that I got heat rash on my face. I ran suicides and carried weights in my backpack. I remembered what L always said, "When you are not working out, the other guy is." I was determined not to be out-worked by anyone.

At eleven, I played in a 13-and-under league. I played with Steve Harley, who went on to play at Nebraska. Steve was considered to have one of the highest basketball IQ's for his age. He really knew the game and that's an area where I was really behind. The highlight of that year was winning the championship game against a team with Chris McCray, who later became one of my best friends and college teammate.

I still lacked confidence, which came from that desire to be liked. When you are too concerned about being liked, you mess up because you are afraid of messing up! Sounds crazy, but it is true. Knowing the game is not the same thing as thinking about every little thing you do on the court. That just leads to more mistakes. You will see how that need to please other people did a lot of harm to me, especially at Maryland.

It was about that time that I noticed something about my game that has stayed with me to this day. I wish I could break out of this pattern, but so far nothing seems to change it. The pattern is that I start out slow every season. I don't know why, but I am glad that I also seem to kick it into gear about mid-season. That has been frustrating for me, and for my coaches, friends, and fans.

The turning point in my confidence came in two tournaments when I was eleven. The first was a 12-and-under tournament in West Virginia. It was the Mountaineer Shootout and for the first time, I was recognized by people who did not know me personally. The thing was though, that they knew of me because Shavery had played in that tournament years before and was great. By the time I left, they would remember me as the tournament MVP!

The second confidence builder was in the Florida Nationals. I played my best basketball yet. I dominated and in one game, I scored 32 points. I was really not aware of how good players are identified for recruiting by colleges at such a young age. I probably didn't even know what the NCAA was, but I liked the attention. After that 32 point performance, some stranger told me, "Son, you are on the NCAA roll book now."

Those two experiences really flipped the switch in me. I was into it now. I worked hard at my game every day all year long. I played in the rain, and I even shoveled snow off the court in the winter so I could shoot around. I just had this adrenalin rush and a burning feeling inside that made me want to get better all the time. I would watch MJ videos and then need to go out and shoot jump shots.

I not only needed to be good, I needed to WIN! But I figured out a couple of other things starting with the reality that being tall does not equal being good. I hated playing smaller players. When you have such a huge height advantage everyone expects you to dominate. If you win, well, you were supposed to, but if you lost, it was, "How could you lose to someone so much shorter than you?"

By seventh grade I entered a pattern that wouldn't change for a long time. I did not pay much attention to school, only to basketball and girls. I played AAU for DC Assault and for the first time really became aware of how far the game of basketball could take me. I noticed more competition to recruit the best players for AAU. One coach, who will remain nameless, showed up one day with six pairs of basketball shoes as an enticement to play for his team.

By eighth grade, I was the second ranked player in the country. A basketball magazine said that I was going to attend Newport High School, which I knew nothing about. Everyone was gunning for me, but I just wanted to go to Suitland High School with my friends. Also, my mom wanted me to get away. She was even checking out coaches. It was all pretty overwhelming.

Mercersburg Academy seemed like a good place to go. They played national powerhouse Oak Hill and they had girls. It would get me away from home, but not too far. So, I took the entrance exam. Well, it might as well have been in another language and my interview was a disaster. That was pretty much it for attending Mercersburg.

I felt bad about Mercersburg. I really wanted to go there. I was practicing with Suitland where the coaches said I would be the man. There was just no way my mom was going to let me go to Suitland High School, so we (well, she) kept looking.

Here I was, a top basketball prospect ranked second in the nation, living twenty minutes from one of the most historic basketball powerhouses in the country and I had never even heard of DeMatha. That was until one day when I was in the basketball gym and my guidance counselor, Mr. Tahir, entered with a pamphlet about DeMatha. He asked me if I ever heard of the school. I said no and asked him a little about it. He told me it was a Catholic school, to which I said I'm not Catholic. The thing that really got me was when he said it was an ALL boys' school. I immediately thought, "Oh no, I will NOT be going there." But he told me how great the school was, and that I needed to check it out.

My mom set up a shadow visit for me. That's a day-long visit so eighth graders can see what the school is all about. My escort was Jordan Collins, who went on to have a great career at North Carolina State, and eventually became a good friend.

Right inside the front door and just outside the gym is a wall with all of the DeMatha Hall of Fame players and coaches from every sport. The main hallway is lined with one long trophy case with photos of the great players in DeMatha history and shelves of trophies.

At one point during the day, I was taken to the athletic offices. The lobby was filled with more trophies—football, basketball, hockey, wrestling, baseball—you name it, DeMatha played it and won championships.

I had a visit with the coaches who would end up having a tremendous impact on my life. I was impressed with Head Coach Morgan Wootten without even really knowing how famous he was. He was really different than coaches from other schools who were recruiting me. I also met with his assistant and son, Joe Wootten, who ended up making sure I took care of business my first year at DeMatha. I then met Neal Murphy. I was to spend a lot of time with "Murph" in my four years there.

I was so unbelievably isolated in Suitland. My visits to Mercersburg and DeMatha were really good for me. I was improving my game, but I was completely unaware of basketball history and what it would mean to play at a place like DeMatha. The biggest thing I remembered about my shadow visit was that I would have to cut my cornrows and no girls!

Walking the hallways with Jordan and meeting all the players made an impression. Catholic Mass, priests, and having religion classes all seemed foreign to me, but the feeling there was totally different than in any school I ever attended. I was pretty impressed with how disciplined everyone seemed and that the guys all got along.

I went to play in the Christmas tournament at DeMatha that year. Then I attended a DeMatha game at the MCI Center, (now the Verizon Center). I had never been at a game with so many fans and the atmosphere was electric. Going to that game did it for me—I wanted to play for DeMatha.

This was when I started learning about the recruiting game. The Suitland coaches, who were so eager to spend time with me before I decided to go to DeMatha, all of a sudden didn't have time for me except for taking one more shot at getting me to change my mind. I was called in to see the coaches one day. They didn't really tell me positive reasons to go to Suitland, they just put down DeMatha saying, "You will never play there."

They weren't bad guys, it's just that coaches have to concentrate on who is going to play for them. They have to develop a strong roster. Everyone is all friendly while they still have a chance to get you, but don't expect a whole lot of love after you make your decision. Remember, it's your life. Don't let yourself be pressured into doing things just to please other people.

On the other side of the coin: coaches who are all sweet and giving you lots of love before you make your choice, get down to business once they know they have you. This is understandable too, but it can be a bit of a shock. I found out fast that being a part of the DeMatha family came with certain expectations. I was told by Coach Wootten that there were certain AAU teams that he did not want me to play for in the summer before my freshman year. He recommended that I play for Coach Wickenhauser in DeMatha's JV summer league, which I did. I was now off and running in my DeMatha career.

FOULS AND FREE THROWS

Criticism and encouragement are a double-double!

Parents: Watch out for coaches that just want to use your child for their own success. There are some out there who want to find good athletes for what they can get from being associated with them. Be involved in what goes on with your kid and the coach. Put your children in situations where they will be able to learn the game while having fun. As they get older there will be plenty of time for the intensity that comes with higher levels of play.

Parents need to be aware of the power they have to encourage and to discourge children in sports. Not every child is blessed with the talent needed to be a great or even a good athlete, but every child can benefit from playing team sports. Make sure your child's coach knows the difference between how to encourage an eight year old and how to motivate a 16 year old.

Parents, particularly of younger players, need to know how coaches use criticism and encouragement. If a coach never points out where a player can improve, then your child will certainly have fun playing, but might not become a better player or teammate. Constructive criticism is a big part of coaching. Sometimes it is hard for parents to hear coaches publicly telling their children what they are doing wrong. As long as a coach is not berating or trying to humiliate a player, don't interfere. Learning to accept criticism and using it to improve as a person and player is part of growing up.

Players: We all have dreams and many of you reading this book want to make it to the professional level or whatever your dream may be. DO NOT allow ANYONE to discourage you and tell you your dreams will never come true. The only one who can determine that is you and God. So strive towards your dreams with 110% effort. Check your motives. Don't pursue a sport just because of the fame and money it may bring. Play because of the love you have for that sport and the desire to compete against the best.

3

Learning from a Legend

DeMatha Basketball

I really had no idea what a big deal it was to play basketball at DeMatha until I got there. It makes a tremendous difference in how you play, and your perception of yourself, when you are surrounded by great coaches, great players, and a great legacy. You either rise to the occasion or sink under the pressure. Luckily for me, I rose to the occasion. Going to DeMatha was the best thing that could have happened to me.

I can tell you honestly that I wasn't too sure about it before I actually got to DeMatha in the fall of 1998. I mean, NO girls? Really? A thousand guys and pretty much every one of us thinking the same thing before our first day—Man, this is NOT a good idea. But it doesn't take long to change your mind and realize there is really no place like DeMatha Catholic High School in academics, athletics, or in brotherhood.

For those who know little or nothing about DeMatha, let me just give you a rundown on just the basketball side of DeMatha history. It all begins with Coach Morgan Wootten. He is one of only three high school coaches who are members of the Basketball Hall of Fame. The High School Player of the Year Award is the Morgan Wootten Award. Coach had an amazing record of 1,274-192. Yeah, you read that right, only 192 losses from 1956 to 2002. I am so grateful that I had the honor to play for him all four years.

Former DeMatha basketball players include Adrian Dantley, Danny Ferry, James Brown of CBS Sports, Keith Bogans, Joseph Forte, Mike Brey, Head Coach of Notre Dame basketball, Kenny Carr, Sid Catlett, Sidney Lowe, and the list goes on. Since the 2002 season, Mike Jones has been the head coach and he has kept DeMatha basketball at the same high level as it was under Coach Wootten. I played for both of these great coaches as well as long-time assistant Neal Murphy.

The same story can be told about the football program. For almost twenty years DeMatha's football program has sent ten or more players to college on full scholarships. At the time I am writing this, DeMatha has more active players in the NFL than any other high school. I am very excited that Elijah Brooks, one of my classmates and close friends, and a star football and basketball player at DeMatha, is now the head football coach at DeMatha! A few years ago, Sports Illustrated magazine started putting out an annual issue with the top twenty-five ranked high school athletic programs. Out of more than 35,000 high schools, DeMatha is ranked in the top three every year.

So now you have an idea what I was walking into. Both Joseph Forte and Keith Bogans were seniors my freshman year at DeMatha. Joe would go on to play at the University of North Carolina. Keith was a star at Kentucky and has had a long NBA career. Even though I played on the JV team that year, I played summer games with them and a lot of scrimmaging. DeMatha sports have always had great senior leadership that passed the legacy of winning championships on to the younger players.

Sometimes the DeMatha "play like a champion" legacy is passed on by the older players in not so friendly ways. I will never forget playing in a summer game with Joe Forte. Jordan Collins scored on me for the game-winning basket. Joe made sure to let me know his disappointment. Now remember, I just came out of the eighth grade and this is the guy that is on his way to UNC to play after his senior year. So, when he looked at me and said, "You're some s**t," I had to either fold up or man up.

I decided to man up. Shoot, what would L and Shavery think if I let myself be intimidated? A few years after that incident, we played against each other in a scrimmage that was watched by a number of college coaches. I was still stinging from Joe's remarks and I used that to motivate me. I played GREAT! Afterward, a big named college coach came up to me and said, "If you keep playing like this, you won't be going to college". He meant that I would be going straight to the NBA from high school.

I know that coach meant well and was probably buttering me up to get a recruiting edge, but young players don't need to hear that kind of thing. The voices that get into our heads and hurt our performances are not always negative. That "can't miss" label is a heavy load. I will have more to say about those voices and labels later, but it is important for you to know that, looking back, it would have been better if he had just said, "Good game". But at the time, I have to admit, I was thrilled and it took the sting out of Joe's words.

Don't misunderstand, what Joe was doing was meant to let me know that poor play is not accepted at DeMatha and that you will be called out on it. It worked and I went on to pass that message to younger players when I was a junior and senior. I may have gone about it differently, but my message was the same—this is DeMatha and you either play hard or you don't play. I know that coaches love when older players take charge and say things that motivate the younger players. Don't be afraid to be a leader.

Now, before we go too far into this, I should tell you that I made some poor decisions when it came to academics in high school. DeMatha is not the kind of place that lets the athletes slide. There are so many great athletes and everyone was expected to do well in the classroom. My problem was that I never really cared about school. That attitude hurt my basketball development and my future ability to relate in other cultures.

So, right off the bat my freshman year, I did what I had always done in the classroom. I did as little as possible. When the six week progress reports came out, guess who was ineligible to play? Right, Travis Garrison. That was a battle I fought during my entire DeMatha career. All I can tell you is that I would have enjoyed high school a lot more if I did three things. First: sit up front in class, second: take notes, and third: do my homework. TRUST ME, those three things are all under your control and life will be a lot easier if you follow those simple steps.

Fortunately, when the time came, I ended up with good enough grades to be eligible for college. DeMatha also has an amazing SAT prep program that was taught for many years by Dr. Buck Offutt who was a lot like Coach Wootten. Both were teachers first and coaches second. That might be hard to believe, but it was true.

Even though I was ultimately able to get the grades I needed, my lack of attention to schoolwork did hurt my basketball development. The reason was pretty simple; I was just too dumb to see it. Every year it was the same thing. I wouldn't work hard in the classroom and ended up having to go to summer school every single summer. That meant that I was unable to work on my basketball skills as much as other players because I was in school all summer.

What really hurt though was all the national exposure I lost from not going to the camps that other elite players were attending. I should have been playing with the Carmelo Anthony's and Amare Stoudemire's rather than sitting in a classroom at DeMatha all summer. It doesn't make sense. If you don't like school then work at it more—not less—during the school year. That way, your summers are free and you are able to do what you love.

Not paying attention to school also hurt me when I became a professional basketball player in Spain. I had to take two years of Spanish at DeMatha, but did not do very well and I did not remember what I learned longer than it took to take the tests. There I was in Spain a few years ago playing professional basketball and unable to speak the language. I was kicking myself for thinking in high school that learning a foreign language was a waste of time. So, TRUST ME, I'm not just repeating the old, "You need an education" line. Seriously, you are only hurting yourself when you do less than your best in school.

Going to DeMatha introduced me to a level of basketball talent and intensity that I had never experienced before. DeMatha is like home base for college coaches when they visit the Washington Metropolitan Area. They know that they can stop in at open gym during the summer and see great players and ones who will one day be great. Open gym is where I first played with guys like Billy Edelin, Andre Scott, Jordan Collins, and Keith Bogans. That is also where I had my encounters with Joe Forte.

I not only had to pick up my intensity, but I had to work even harder. I never had a problem with hard work on the basketball court, but I also had to learn how to work smart. Before I got to DeMatha, my idea of working on my game was pretty much just taking a lot of different shots. I soon learned that practicing shots is only one part of improving your game.

One of the great things about hanging around DeMatha open gym is that you randomly run into former players like the great Adrian Dantley. You find out that you are in a family now that looks out for each other. It was Adrian Dantley who took me aside that first summer and asked me what the first thing was that I should do when I go on a court. I probably said something like layups or shoot around. He shook his head and said, "Drills."

It was as simple as that, but it was new to me. This was one of the greatest scorers in the game and his advice to me was not about shooting, but about doing drills. That's what I mean by not just working hard, but working smart. It was all pretty overwhelming, but I knew I was at the right place even before I started my freshman year.

My mom knew I was in the right place, too. Great coaches know that you recruit a player's mom as much as you recruit the player. That is even true at the college level. My mom loved Coach Wootten. She didn't know anything about basketball but whatever Coach said was gospel to her. She knew he wanted the best for me.

I played JV my freshman year for Coach Tom Burke. Mr. Burke was in charge of discipline for the school so a lot of guys only knew that side of him; but he was a great coach. There are certain things that young players need to learn before they can move up and make an impact at a higher level. Warren Williams and I were two of the players who would go on to be star players on the DeMatha varsity, but we really learned a lot that first year from Coach Burke.

The purpose of JV and freshman basketball at DeMatha is to introduce players to the DeMatha system. That includes the expectation to win and to win a lot. The JV only lost one game that season and I will always be grateful to Coach Burke for the encouragement he gave me. He was always honest in his evaluation of the players and he would let you know how you were doing. It meant a lot to me when he would say that he was seeing me improve.

I was also finding out that first year that it is not so bad being at an all-boys school. Not that I wouldn't have loved to be going to a school with girls, but look: anywhere you have a thousand teenage boys, the girls will find you. It is hard to explain the sense of brotherhood that begins to develop right away at DeMatha. I have made friends everywhere I have been, but my classmates and teammates at DeMatha will always be special.

By mid-year, I was surviving in the classroom and thriving on the court so life was good. The laughter and joking in the lunchroom and the friendships that were formed are things I will never forget. Believe it or not, I also go back to see some of my teachers. As hard as it was for me academically, the teachers and staff there really care about the students.

It won't surprise anyone familiar with DeMatha that my favorite classroom teacher was Mr. Machesky. He has a way of making history really interesting. I recently learned that he was named Private School Teacher of the Year by the Washington Post. I believe it, he had a big impact on me and I am grateful to him and to all my teachers for doing more than just "getting me through."

There were also people on the administrative level like the principle, John Moylan, who came to DeMatha in the 1950's about the same time as Coach Wootten and Buck Offutt. Between them, they had almost 150 years of service to DeMatha. But there is one person that I can honestly say is the reason I made it at DeMatha, and that's Mrs. Guerin. She was the greatest tutor and academic advisor ever. She loved every single DeMatha student and believed in us like you can't imagine. Thanks Mrs. Guerin, I and a lot of other DeMatha men owe our academic success to you.

The summer before my sophomore year was pretty amazing. I was able to work as a referee at Coach Wootten's basketball camp at Mount St. Mary's. This is one of the most famous basketball camps in the country and it draws great players. In the evenings, some of the DeMatha players and others would play pick-up games. This was another time that the older players were very demanding. It made me think back to my days of playing with my older brothers and all their friends. No one took it easy on me then or at Coach Wootten's camp.

I was ready to be a big part of the team and expectations were high. Billy Edelin, Ben Gordon, and I went to the Junior Olympics in France that summer as well. I was becoming a lot more aware of the bigger basketball universe. I had been so isolated before going to DeMatha and now I could see that basketball was an international game. Since my arrival at DeMatha, I had been seeing truly great players and I was determined that I would soon be recognized as one of them.

This was when I first sensed that it meant something to be Travis Garrison. I don't mean that in an arrogant way, but there comes a time that you have to figure out who you are and who you want to be. I knew I wanted my name to mean something.

Bogans and Forte had moved on and Billy and Jordan Collins were now the leaders. Warren Williams and I moved up to the varsity and I got my first day-in, day-out exposure to Coach Wootten and the varsity staff. I guess I was not as confident as I thought because it seemed like I was always apologizing whenever I did something wrong, even missing a shot.

Remember, I was the little boy who always wanted people to like him. That's why I felt like I had to be perfect and in sports, just like in life, that is impossible. As long as I was playing just to avoid mistakes I would never be a good player, let alone achieve greatness. Playing not to make mistakes limits you to being average. Do not be self-conscious about making mistakes. You will make them and you will learn from them. You have to be confident and take risks. But most importantly, when you miss that shot or commit a dumb foul, forget about it. Do not allow it to keep you from being confident and taking more risks.

It got so bad during the season that I wouldn't shoot. There are two extremes, guys who just catch-and-shoot all the time and then there was me. I had the catch-and-pass-it mentality. It was making Coach Wootten crazy. He had coached players with this problem before; there was nothing Coach had not seen in almost fifty years of coaching. He and the other coaches just hung in there, encouraged me to stop apologizing all the time and just play my game.

What they were trying to get through to me was to take that confidence that I had off the court and let it come out on the court. Be the man. What finally did it was a game against Archbishop Carroll High School. The day before the game, in practice, I was consistently catching the ball and immediately passing it. Coach Wootten blew his whistle, stopped practice, and walked over to me. He told me that every time I caught the ball near the free throw line, I had his permission to shoot. It seems that was all I needed because, to everyone's amazement including my own, the next day at the game I took the last shot for the game winner. Good, right? Well, I missed and even though Coach was not happy about losing, he let me know that he liked that I took the last shot. That meant a lot to me and from that point on, it changed the way I played at DeMatha.

I finished my sophomore year on a high note with a 22-point performance against McNamara in a playoff game. We lost to St. Johns in the conference championship but I had figured out who I was that season. That was when I went from being Travis Garrison in my mind to being Travis Garrison on the court and I was just getting started. I got my first college letter after my sophomore season. It was from LaSalle and I was so naïve that I was ready to commit to them right then and there.

I can't emphasize enough the importance of players and parents learning as much as they can about the larger basketball world. Here I was in my second year at DeMatha and I had so little understanding of big-time college basketball that I was ready to commit to LaSalle just because they sent one letter. I didn't even know which conference they played in, but it would not have mattered if I did. I still didn't know much about the NCAA or the differences between the conferences. I couldn't have told you that the ACC was better than the Atlantic-10.

If recruiters are going to learn everything they can about you, you need to know everything you can about them. You need to investigate the recruiting process and the culture and history of the game. You have to know the larger basketball world and how things work outside of your personal circles. I had friends who were football players who knew tons more about the best college basketball players and the best teams than I did. All I knew was "Be like Mike" and that really was it.

The summer before my junior year, I played in some pick-up games hosted by Keith "The Shot Doc" Veney. He was well respected in the basketball community and players from the NBA, top colleges, and some who played overseas, would come out to play in his games. The games were tough and intense, but really helped to boost my confidence as a player. No fouls were called unless the defense called the foul. It was very competitive basketball, which made playing high school basketball easier for me.

We were looking good for my junior year, but we lost Billy Edelin before the season started. Billy had averaged almost 20 points the season before, but ended up having to leave DeMatha. I also gained Mike Anderson as a mentor. Mike was a two-time All-Met tailback for DeMatha football and went on to play at the University of Maryland where he overcame chronic myelogenous leukemia. Mike was like a big brother to me and I will always be grateful to him.

Sometime during my junior year the rumors began to grow that Coach Wootten would retire. I don't know how much that affected us as a team, but we were assured he was going to stay and coach. That season started off rough, but we still had a lot of talented players. We were not playing well at all the first half of the season. We went to the Beach Ball Classic in South Carolina and lost in a big upset to a small school that had Raymond Felton, who went on to play for University of North Carolina and the New York Knicks. We dropped in the rankings. ESPN High School Sports reported, "Travis Garrison scored just two points in the loss to Latta, as DeMatha tumbles 11 spots this week." Coach was VERY upset, and showed it in practice the following day.

I was having some pretty serious anger issues on the court. When things did not go my way, I would explode. I went after refs, opponents, whoever. The player I really wanted to be like was Kevin Garnett. He always played with a lot of passion and emotion on the court and I tried to be just like him. It really came to a head in a regular season loss to McNamara. I was mouthing off the whole game and eventually was given a technical foul. Coach Wootten came to my defense and also got a technical called on him.

Coach always protected his players, but he was not happy with me. This was a man who never raised his voice. He knew how to use sarcasm. In four years, I never once heard him raise his voice. So here I am playing for the great Morgan Wootten and acting like an ass on the court. The technical foul hurt the team, but Coach Wootten knew that this was about a lot more than just one game.

In the locker room, Coach let us have it. He said, "Some people should just join a debate team because all they want to do is talk." I knew he was referring to me. After he met with the team, he pulled me aside and just said, "Let the scoreboard do the talking." That's it. Coach didn't have to tell me twice. I didn't talk again and, surprise, we did not lose another game all season! How many coaches can say one thing and make that happen?

We had won the WCAC (Washington Catholic Athletic Conference) championship and were preparing for the City Title Game against the District of Columbia Public Schools champions, Spingarn High School. We had a senior point guard that year named Zach Clark. Zach is one of the most inspirational people I have ever met. He played a big part in our success that year.

There was a pretty heated press conference the week of the game. The Spingarn players thought that DeMatha was soft. That's kind of the way it goes when a private school plays a public school. Because of my past and just my pride as an athlete, I did not like all the talk about being soft. The results of the game at the MCI Center were DeMatha 69 Spingarn 50. I had 25 points, 7 rebounds and was named MVP. So, just like Coach told me, I let the scoreboard do the talking.

FOULS AND FREE THROWS

Check out coaches and teams before committing!

Parents: The teen years are a time that SOME AAU coaches and SOME high school coaches and SOME people want to be around your child for the wrong reasons. Sometimes their own ambition gets in the way of doing what is best for your child. You have to be able to weave out the good from the bad because they are not all bad or all good. There are some people and coaches that see all the potential in kids and just want to help them reach that potential. You have to be careful who you allow to have influence over your children.

You are giving your children to coaches for several hours a day. If you are working full-time, that may be more time than you spend with them. Do your homework! There are some VERY good talkers out here. If there is someone that is taking a strong interest in your child, ask around about him or her, get some background information about this person before you allow him or her into your child's life.

Good coaches let players know that they care, but no two coaches communicate caring in the same way. What you want in a coach is the ability to critique a player without breaking his spirit. Coaches will often say, "As long as I am being hard on you, everything is fine. When I stop being tough on you, then you should worry." Other coaches might be more traditional about expressing their care for the player with pats on the back or always following criticism with some encouragement. Most coaching staffs have both types and that's a good combination. But good coaches know that if you never communicate in a positive way that you care, some kids will just shut down physically and emotionally.

Players: You have to educate yourself about the larger world of basketball. You have to learn about the best coaches and the best AAU teams. If you aren't going to public school, then find the best private school programs. Do the same for college and then in getting an agent and learning how the world of professional sports works. Otherwise, there will be people who will take advantage of you.

4

Travis Garrison

McDonald's All-American

I went into the summer before my senior year on the momentum of the City Title Game against Spingarn. I had not really appreciated before what it meant to win the WCAC championship and to be the individual MVP. Our conference has always been considered one of the best in the country so colleges really pay attention to the top players. We often traveled to tournaments across the country and beat nationally ranked teams, only to come back and lose to a conference rival.

I was named All-Met and All-State and I was not close to being satisfied. The individual awards were great and I was honored to receive them, but I have always been about team accomplishments so I never let it go to my head. Coach Wootten wouldn't have let that happen anyway, he preached team, team, and team all the time.

The summer of 2001 I was invited to the ABCD Adidas Camp even though I was a NIKE guy, meaning that I had always played for a NIKE-sponsored AAU team. This was the first camp for elite players I had ever attended. The other guys there went to these kinds of camps every year. People had heard about me, but had never seen me play. Remember, while everyone else was getting exposure at these camps, I was in summer school making up for not working hard during the school year. Do you see why that matters now?

Guys like Carmelo Anthony, LeBron James, and Chris Bosh were there and I wanted to prove something. Everyone knew each other except me because I never came out until now. I had to stand out and make an impression and I did. I made the best of it that week and was named to the All-Star team, but could not play in the game because I had to get back for summer school again.

After that week I was on everyone's Top 25 Players list. ESPN called me the next Shane Battier. Recruiting went off the charts. I was really feeling it now. This was my moment, my time. I went into my senior season with the attitude that I was for real and we were going to dominate as a team. Our goal was to not lose even one game, not even in summer league.

We played in two different summer leagues. In the first, we met our goal and did not lose one game. In the second, we won all of our games until we got to the championship game against Oxon Hill. We lost to them after beating them by 15 in the regular season. I was so upset and disappointed by our loss that I didn't want to play in the summer league All-Star game. But we all worked hard that summer. Coach Jones trained us in the old hot gym at DeMatha and we were in great shape.

I was playing with a chip on my shoulder for a lot of reasons. One was that a player at the ABCD camp that I had gone to said that we will lose to his team during the season. He played for one of the top six ranked teams in the country and we were scheduled to play them in a tournament in Massachusetts. I wasn't going to let that happen.

I put on a show every game for all the college coaches who attended open gym at DeMatha that summer. Three years prior to this an ACC coach said to me, "We want you really bad, but if you keep playing like this, you won't be going to college." Again, I was flattered, but putting thoughts of the NBA in my head at that point was not the best thing a coach could do.

As I have said before, you can get just as distracted by voices in your head that are telling you how great you are as you can by critical voices. Constant praise can give you a warped sense of reality. It was hard to keep that "never satisfied" attitude when I found out that an NBA scout said that I had "a huge upside." When you get great compliments on your skills and your game, it's important to keep your ego in check.

On the other hand, negative criticism might actually be a blessing in disguise. For instance, one trainer who had thought highly of my game before meeting me, worked me out and said, "He has no skills." Situations such as these can help keep you humble, but again, you can't allow them to affect your thinking either. My point being, that whatever the feedback is—whether good or bad—that you take it with a grain of salt and try to use it as motivation without allowing it to affect the way you see yourself or your game.

In September 2001, I committed to play for Gary Williams at the University of Maryland. I was one of four freshmen they signed that year. Shortly after that week I played in the Charlie Weber Invitational, a tournament played at the University of Maryland, and made the All-Tournament team.

Travis and Corey McCrae with their parents on signing day

My personal goal that season was to be named a McDonald's All-American. I knew that meant that I had to play well especially in out of town games. I was named MVP of every tournament in which we played. One of those was the Hall of Fame Tournament in Massachusetts. Remember the player from the ABCD Camp who said his team would beat us in that tournament? Well, when the game arrived, I made sure it was all business. It turned out we didn't face them until the championship game, and we ended up winning by about 15 points. As tempting as it was to rub it in his face, I replayed Coach's advice in my head and just let the scoreboard do the talking.

We were a confident team and we had great leadership from the coaching staff and the seniors. I wish I had written down all of the quotes from Coach Wootten that season. He gave us a new quote every single day. His most famous saying was, "Class gets you to the top; character keeps you there." How many programs, players, and coaches have spent years building a first class program or personal reputation only to have it collapse because of a lack of character?

One of my best friends and one of the finest leaders I have ever known was our point guard Elijah Brooks. I was always a quiet leader, but Elijah had no problem getting in your face. He had just led the football team to an undefeated record and 22 straight wins over two seasons. It's no surprise to any of his classmates that he is now the head football coach at DeMatha. We didn't know it then, but we were going to be part of one of the greatest classes in the history of DeMatha athletics.

We only lost three games throughout my entire senior season. We played in five tournaments and won them all. Most importantly, we won the WCAC championship and the City Title Game. I was named first team All-Met by the Washington Post, the Gazette Player of the Year, and Maryland's Gatorade Player of the Year. Even with all of my awards and accomplishments, I was deeply disappointed that I was not named All-Met Player of the Year. There are two ways to go with our disappointments, one is to fold or blame other people. The other way is to be a man and realize that some things are out of our control.

I do not know what else I could have done as an individual or team player, but I had to live with the decision and not let it spoil a great senior year. What hurt me just as much was that DeMatha was ranked number two in the area by the Washington Post. That one no one understands, but we still all celebrated a great season.

I received two other honors that mean a lot to me to this day. The first was being named a McDonald's All-American. I learned from Coach Wootten that team goals come first, but I had set this as my number one individual goal and it was very satisfying to achieve it. It meant that I would be going to play in Madison Square Garden with the top players in the country. The second was being invited to play in the Michael Jordan's first All-Star game. To be associated in any way to the name of Michael Jordan is an honor that few high school players ever experience.

Travis and Michael Jordan at the Jordan Brand Classic All-Star game

Remember the subtitle of the book is "An Athlete's Battle" and that my toughest opponent was my own self-doubt. You are probably wondering how this fits in right here since this seems like the highest point that any high school player can reach, right? I was All-Met, a McDonald's All-American, a Jordan All-Star and I was headed to the University of Maryland to play for the National Champions.

It is an amazing fact, but as soon as I was named to the McDonald's All-American Team the critics came out in force. They said I didn't deserve it, that Coach Wootten had too much influence and got me in, and that I was not the caliber of the other players. TRUST ME, if you let the sports writers, bloggers and sports board fans get into your head, you will regret it. Whether what they say is good or bad, take it all with the attitude that you don't measure yourself by their opinions of you.

So, once again, I was off to prove myself, this time in the greatest sports arena in the world, Madison Square Garden. How good are McDonald's All-Americans? In an ironic twist for my life, every college team to win the NCAA men's championship since 1978 had at least one McDonald's All-American on its roster, except for, you guessed it, the 2002 Maryland Terps.

Amare Stoudemire, Carmelo Anthony, Chris Bosh, and J.J. Reddick are just a few of the players who I met when I showed up at the Garden. I was extremely nervous. I wanted to show everyone that I belonged, but I only scored two points. It was hard to have reached my goal of being a McDonald's All-American only to leave the game feeling that I had not showcased my talents.

Travis and the legendary Hall of Fame college coach John Wooden

The week after the game at the Garden, I played in the Jordan All-Star game at the Verizon Center. Except for Chris Bosh, it was all the same top players, but this time I showed up to play. I wasn't nearly as nervous. First, I guess because I had already been through this once before. Second, the Verizon Center felt like home. For some reason, the same Travis Garrison who only scored two points in Madison Square Garden, scored 16 points the second time around. It did not get the same publicity, but at least all those great players saw what I could do.

Around that same time, Coach Wootten announced that the 2001-02 season was his last as the head coach for DeMatha. It was one of the greatest honors of my life to play on Coach Wootten's last DeMatha team. Coach would be known as a winner no matter what kind of season we had, but we were thrilled to be able to give him a terrific season as a way of saying thank you for all that he did for hundreds of DeMatha players over the years.

I have said several times to be careful what voices you let inside your head. Coach Wootten's voice is one that I always want to hear in my head. He gave me a tremendous compliment at the end of the season. The greatest basketball coach ever told USA Today, "Out of the 13 players that I have coached who went on to the play in the NBA, Travis Garrison is in the top six." Even to this day, I value his opinion and insight when it comes to life and the game of basketball.

Thanks Coach Wootten and thanks to everyone at DeMatha for four unforgettable years.

Travis, Father Albert, and Corey McCrae at
DeMatha graduation June 2002

FOULS AND FREE THROWS

Work hard on your weaknesses!

Players: Work on your skills to get even better at the things you already do well, but don't forget about also working on your weaknesses. What you can't do on the court or in life can hurt you. Your strengths are not always enough to get you to victory. Spend more time working on the things you are not good at than on the things you already know how to do well.

Do not be a know-it-all because you don't! Even the best players in the world do not know everything and are always learning something new. Always be open to listening to people's advice whether you think you need to or not. Some things you may already know and some things you could be hearing for the first time. Not all advice is good advice, but at least hear what people you trust have to say.

One of the most important keys to being a good, and even great player, is to be coachable and a hard worker. Coaches LOVE those two characteristics, TRUST ME. Be a player coaches do not have to tell to go out and work hard, or put some extra time in before or after practice. Be one of those players that a coach brags about; telling people how hard of a worker you are, how they LOVE coaching you. Be that kind of player.

Whether you are up or down, always be humble. It's good to be extremely confident on the court or field, but be modest about praising yourself, let others do that. If you are good enough, the praise will come. If you can be humble while everything is going great, then when things are not going so well, people won't be so hard on you.

I got it in my mind that I was not a post player. When I got to Maryland, Coach Williams pushed me and even made me angry with his insistence that I work on my inside game. It does not really matter whether I am a post player or not; what matters is that a coach wanted me to increase and improve the skills that I brought to the game. No one likes to practice their weak areas, but a coach who drives you to improve every aspect of your game is really doing you a favor in the long run, TRUST ME.

5

Swagger and Self-Doubt

Maryland Terps

I moved on campus right after I graduated from DeMatha. I wanted to be totally prepared for the season. My NBA dreams were waiting and I wanted to dominate right from the beginning. The only problem was that all this freedom gave me more time than I needed to prepare for basketball. It was not a good situation for me that summer, living in the dorm and being within walking distance of way too many bars and clubs. I was a Maryland Terrapin now, playing basketball and having fun. I had a girlfriend and was partying almost every night.

My mindset was that I would be at Maryland for one or two years and then it was onto the NBA. My goal was not to get a college degree; it was to make it to the NBA. I know now that was the wrong attitude to have about my college career and it wasn't even the best attitude to have to get to the NBA. It was especially unfair to Coach Williams and my Maryland teammates.

Jonathan Hargett was potentially the first point guard that would be taken by the NBA out of high school. He was only five-foot six-inches with incredible explosiveness, and had a lot of game. Jonathan and I were caught up in an unexpected controversy before school even started. He and I were under investigation by the NCAA for our association with Mike Anderson. Mike Anderson had been my mentor for two years and our relationship was never about him being affiliated with a financial group. That didn't matter to the NCAA. As soon as I was at an NCAA school, Mike became an associate of a financial group first and foremost, not a mentor.

I was cleared of any wrong doing, but that did not make the front page of the sports section like the initial investigation. The only thing that some people knew about me was that I was being investigated. I knew that I had not done anything wrong, but it was the wrong message to send to the coaching staff, my teammates, the fans, and the press.

I worked hard that summer at two things, basketball and having fun. I was one of five highly sought after recruits to sign with the NCAA National Champions. It was John Gilchrist, Chris McCray, Nik Caner-Medley, junior college transfer Jamar Smith, and me. We were hot, not just locally, but the national sports press touted us as the "freshmen fearsome foursome" coming in as Maryland reloaded for another championship run.

Also during that summer, I became close with Alpha Bangura who played at St. John's College in New York at the time. Alpha had a great work ethic; bazaar might be a good word for it. We shared our dreams with each other that summer. We worked out together a lot, and he showed me what it would take for me to be ready for the college level. We were brothers and I could really talk to him. He was both a friend and a motivator. We all need guys like that in our lives. Make sure you have someone around you who will talk straight with you.

I had classes at Maryland that summer, too, but I did what I always did in school, which was as little as possible. I went to class only because I had too. I stayed on the upper-class side of campus to be with the action and went to the bars and clubs almost every night. I was living off the hype of being Travis Garrison; not the quiet, hardworking, all-basketball-all-the-time Travis. Nope, this was the new Travis Garrison, burning the candle at both ends.

When school started in August, nothing changed except there were more girls on campus and more action. I look back now and realize that the first two weeks of school that year were really the beginning of the end for me at Maryland. I would be there for all four years, but once this craziness began, it really had a life of its own and never ended. If I had stopped right then, everything could have been different, but I was living the life and wanted it all. I take full responsibility for my destructive attitude and behavior.

I was young enough so that I could stay up all night, go to some classes, work out during the day and just start all over. So, when Midnight Madness came around November 1, I was already known as a partier and big drinker. But that night at Comcast Center when I was introduced with the team to the fans for the first time, I was flying. I had never experienced anything like that in my life.

My freshman year was pretty uneventful. I was learning to play as a 4-5. That's basketball talk for power forward and center. I like to play the 3, but Coach Williams had other plans, so when my freshman year was just so-so, everyone—including me—chalked it up to the transition to college basketball and playing a different position.

Meanwhile, Carmelo Anthony was up at Syracuse winning an NCAA National Championship and becoming a first round draft pick as a freshman. So, while I was using being a freshman as an excuse, Melo was having none of that. He was ballin' and getting it done. Being a freshman to him was an opportunity and to me it was an excuse. That doesn't mean that I could have been as good as Melo just because I wanted to, but it does mean that I could have paid more attention to basketball and less to partying and maybe, just maybe, things would have turned out differently for me in the long run.

I trained hard that summer following my freshman year. Chris McCray and I went to Croatia to play in a tournament put together by other collegiate basketball players to compete with professional Eastern European teams. Interestingly, I ended up spending years playing professionally in Eastern Europe. To get ready for my sophomore year, I also trained that summer with basketball skills trainer Idan Raven, who trained a lot of NBA guys.

Going into my sophomore year I knew I was going to be starting with the three other sophomores and senior Jamar Smith. There was a huge buildup around Maryland starting four sophomores; this was supposed to be our breakout year.

I had gained about 10 good solid pounds, I felt great, and looked as big and strong as could be. Once again: no reason to focus on my education when I would be in the NBA by this time next year. TRUST ME, as I was soon to find out, that was a foolish attitude.

I still was not comfortable as a 4-5. Gary was on me a lot. I even got kicked out of practice a few times. That's how Gary coaches. Either you are going to do it his way or you are out. That was a lot different than what I was used to with Coach Wootten. I can't count how many people have tried to make excuses for my performance at Maryland by saying that it was Gary's fault for not letting me play my game. Others said that I should have gone to school somewhere that had an offense more suited to my skills.

On the one hand, I understand and appreciate their point. I had some of the same thoughts at that time; but that kind of thinking ignores a lot of reality. First, when a player commits to playing basketball for a school and a coach, he has an obligation to fit into that system and not keep fighting and butting heads with the coach for four years. Which was what I, unfortunately, pretty much had done. Second, Gary was right to push me to improve my inside skills. A coach that lets you just work on your strengths is not doing you any favors, especially if your goal is to make it to the NBA where the more skills you have the better your chances of success.

There was a lot of hype and excitement when I was a freshman, but no real pressure. Whatever happened that year was overlooked because we were young. But with so many great players leaving school early for the NBA, sophomores are no longer considered young and I was feeling the pressure. Being the McDonald's All-American was both a blessing and a burden. There is nowhere to hide from the expectations that go with that title.

I became my biggest critic. I no longer had that DeMatha swagger, the "I'm Travis Garrison and I'm going to dominate you" attitude that was more confidence than arrogance. I knew Gary wanted me to play inside with my back to the basket; so I was always worried now about taking jump shots. My strength had become a psychological barrier.

When a jump shooter is making his shots, there is no thinking. The mind has already done its work in thinking about correct form and focus during the tens of thousands of practice shots he has taken over the years. Great shooters are mindless. The worst thing that can happen to a shooter is to be consciously thinking about how he is shooting the ball.

Worse than thinking about how you are shooting is having your mind on the bench and what the coach is thinking as you go up for the shot. That's really deadly for a shooter.

I am sure you have heard someone say about a shooter who is knocking down every shot that, "He's unconscious." Well, that's actually true in a way because I know when I am really on, I am not conscious of all the little things that I do to make a great jump shot. Once I decide to take the shot my mind shuts off, I trust my instincts. Unfortunately, I stopped doing that and as I was going up for shots most of my sophomore year, my mind was wondering what Gary was thinking.

Any of you who remember me that year know that I was up and down. Good game or two then disappear. That's what happened in a game in Gainesville when we were playing the number one ranked team in the country, the Florida Gators. I missed so many layups it was embarrassing. Now I was even self-conscious about the easiest shot in basketball. I had a terrible game that I am now remembered for as a hero because of what happened at the end.

We were down by one and the ball came to me. I just wanted to pass the ball, but I was too open. I was scared, truly petrified, but somehow I got the shot off. Normally, being that scared would mean an automatic miss, but not this time, this time the ball went in to clinch the game. The Maryland band and the fans back home, as I found out later, went crazy. I went into the locker room after the game and cried, not tears of joy, tears about how terribly I had played.

For all of the sports writers who wrote hurtful things about me: I can tell you, I understood your frustration with me more than you can imagine. I deserved the criticism for how I was playing, but sometimes writers like to think they know what is going on inside you to make you do what you do. They might guess right some of the time, but it's only a lucky guess. No one really knows what is going on in anyone else's mind and heart.

I was lost. One game Coach Williams described me on the court as a deer caught in the headlights. Fear of failure and of doing something that Gary or my teammates or the fans would criticize paralyzed me. I was devastated at how I was playing. And because I want young players to learn from my mistakes, I have to be brutally honest and say that win or lose, I could still be found in the clubs having a good time. I was usually alone, hardly ever with my teammates, they weren't responsible for my performances or for the fact that I was still running around partying.

Right before the ACC tournament, we beat N.C. State in a big game. We needed to do well in the tournament because we were "on the bubble" for the NCAA tournament. March Madness was coming and we were in danger of not even getting in just two years after winning it all. In a moment of inspiration that came from somewhere, I sat alone and watched myself in an old DeMatha game tape. It was like watching another person. It was obvious how much fun I was having and just dominating the game.

I was determined that no matter what happened, I was at least going to have fun playing. So, game one of the ACC tournament, we beat Chris Paul's Wake Forest team. I had 17 points and 10 rebounds. I don't know how long it had been since I had a double-double, but I was having fun and it felt great. Then we beat N.C. State in the second game, mostly because of John Gilchrist's unbelievable performance.

We had entered the tournament as the sixth seed and beat the second and third seeds to get to the championship against Duke. Duke had won the last five ACC Tournaments titles. We took the Blue Devils to overtime and won 95-87. I had 19 points and was named to the second team All-Tournament team and John Gilchrist won the MVP award.

Maryland had only won the ACC tournament championship twice before and not since 1984, 20 years before. We came into the tournament hoping to win at least two games and hoped to get into the NCAA Tournament. Winning the championship gave us an automatic bid. We won our first round game, but lost by two to defending National Champion Syracuse Orange Men. I had 16 points and seven rebounds. I was having fun again and got my swagger back. Don't ever lose sight that this is the game we love and that enjoying it is also the best way to be successful.

John Gilchrist and Travis celebrating Maryland's first ACC Tournament Championship in twenty years

The summer after my sophomore year, I went to a camp to train with some NBA players in Las Vegas. After that, I went with the Terps to Italy to play against some international pro teams. I played very well in Vegas and in Italy and my confidence was sky high. I was ready for my junior year as the "fearsome foursome" was coming back.

Looking back, I know that I was more balanced as a person than I was in my first two years. The swagger was back, I was having fun again like I used to at DeMatha and I was working out after practice in a way I had never done before. Still, I have to be honest and admit that I didn't have that obsessive drive that it takes to achieve greatness.

Balance is fine if you just want to be average, but most people who have attained greatness have an obsessive commitment to their area of interest. I mean, if I was going to be balanced, I should have been balanced between basketball and academics. I was balanced between playing basketball and partying and it showed on the court.

The season began and I went back to that same up and down way of playing. Showing up one game and then disappearing. Gary was subbing me out more and more and there were untrue rumors that I was considering transferring out. Even though it was not true, people would talk to me like it was a fact and tell me that I needed to get out of Gary's system, play somewhere else.

Although things were not great between Gary and me, I didn't allow myself to get caught up in the finger-pointing. Of course I wasn't happy about my playing time and we butted heads a lot in my career at Maryland. I was just so stubborn and wanted to do things my way, thinking I knew it all. I am not saying that I did not sometimes wish I was somewhere else, but I was only twenty years old and I was not playing well. I was the "can't miss" kid and my mind was spinning.

We lost in the first round of the ACC Tournament in our hometown at the Verizon Center that year. We were going to the NIT (National Invitational Tournament) and not the NCAA. We played well for a few games and made it to the semi-finals. We played the semi-final in Madison Square Garden in New York. Near the end of the game, we were losing. I was at the foul line shooting a free throw and a kid in Maryland gear in the stands behind the basket stood up, pointed at me and yelled so everyone could hear, "Garrison, you suck!"

Fans have the right to say whatever they want within reason and that was not over the line, but it hurt. I was watching my dreams slip away and was angry at myself for letting it happen. When you pay good money to watch a game, you can do what that kid did and everyone thinks it's no big deal as though the players aren't human beings. I can't deny that my play sucked and I did not look like a McDonald's All-American. That fan was not the enemy, the enemy was inside me. It was my own self-doubt standing up and shouting, "Travis Garrison, you suck."

I thought about declaring for the NBA draft that spring, but decided against it. There was no buzz and I knew if I had a great senior year, I could still live my dream. John Gilchrist left for the NBA and I re-committed myself to finding my game, to being Travis Garrison again and going out on a high note.

I watched players get drafted that spring who I knew did not have as much talent as I had. It motivated me to buckle down and train that summer like never before. I had my knee scoped after the season, after attending Baron Davis's Camp in L.A. Because of this I didn't stay long to participate at the camp. But the message I got from NBA insiders that summer was that I needed to average double-doubles to have a chance to be drafted. I knew the real Travis Garrison could do that if I could just find him again.

FOULS AND FREE THROWS

Communicate! Communicate! Communicate!

Parents: Communicate! Even though your children act like they are all grown up, they still need you. Even the ones "on their own" in college need you to communicate that you are there to listen whenever they need to talk. I know I had a lot of things going on inside of me long after I was out of college that I needed to talk about.

Kids need to talk at the strangest times. They may say things are "fine", but dig a little, things may not be fine. So no matter how annoyed they might seem, check in with them. Your child's life outside of your home, especially college, is a whole other world.

Encourage your children to communicate with their coaches. Every parent needs other adult voices telling their children what kids sometimes shut out when it comes from parents. Provided you have done a good job of finding coaches who care about their players, which most do, then a coach can be a tremendous influence on your child.

Just as parents need to be aware that their children have a lot of things going on both on and off the court, coaches need to be aware that their players are bringing what's happening at home to the court. When something at home is really affecting your child, it might be helpful for his coaches to know about it. That's your call and all you can do is decide what is best for your child. Just remember that most coaches are grateful for any information that will help them coach your child to perform better.

Players: Communicate! Talk to the people who care about you. Let them know what is bothering you. When I was at my lowest point, I went to see an elder in my church. He really helped me. Coaches also want you at your best and if you let them know that you are hurting about something at home or in school, they will surprise you with how much they care. By the time I was at Maryland, my head was full of every negative word said about me in the papers, on blogs, TV and radio, and from friends, family, and Maryland fans. Those words were turning into self-doubts and affecting my play. Having coaches to talk to really helps; let them know what's bothering you. Communicate!

Had I told Coach Williams or one of his assistants that I was struggling with regaining my confidence, we could have started a dialogue that could have led to some things changing. It takes courage to tell people that you are struggling, but it shows that you care about playing at your best and being a good person when you can open up to people who care about you.

6

Losing it All

Bad Decisions

October 2005 was not the best month for Maryland athletics. The incident in the bar that would eventually lead to my arrest in January was not yet public knowledge, but I wasn't the only Maryland athlete getting into trouble that month. The Washington Post reported that:

> Three [Terps] football players participated in a bar fight at the Cornerstone Grill & Loft....The three football players were each suspended for one game...and received an official letter of probation from the athletic department.

In reaction to this incident, Coach Williams immediately banned the basketball team from going to bars for the season. Although I did not know it at the time, my life had changed forever. The sad part is that everything would have been different if I had kept my commitment to myself to not hang out at the bars. It should not have taken a ban from Coach to keep me out of trouble.

During the summer, I had written down in detail all of my goals for school and basketball in the 2005-2006 school year. I had three categories, school goals, basketball goals and "things I have to do to achieve my goals." My goals in the classroom were pretty simple, but not easy. I didn't just want to avoid failing any classes, but to get no less than a C in every class. The second goal was to have only eleven credits remaining for graduation by the end of the year.

My basketball goals were to:

1. Get in great shape and stay in great shape
2. Average at least 14 points and eight rebounds a game
3. Win the ACC regular season and tournament
4. Help lead the team to another NCAA Championship
5. Leave a team legacy of being the Maryland team that went through adversity and finished on top
6. Be remembered as a great Maryland player
7. Put myself in a position to be drafted in the top 20 of the first round of the NBA draft

Things I had to do to achieve my goals:

1. No going out
2. No drinking
3. Stay after practice for extra shots
4. Workout at night instead of going out
5. Stay focused

In big letters at the bottom of the page, I wrote:

GOD 1ST & SACRIFICE

Many of the McDonald's All-Americans that I played with three years before were getting ready to start their NBA careers. Carmelo Anthony was already in his third year. I was ready to make my own run for the NBA draft; I was motivated, but I had to get off to a good start and get that swagger back.

I had stuck to my commitment of not going to bars or hanging out at night. I had done everything I could to prepare myself. I didn't see any harm in going out one time when I just needed to get out a little, socialize, and relax. Also, my need to be liked was still lingering. It was important to me to be seen as an approachable, good guy and I thought the best way to do that is to socialize at the bar with my fellow students. So, I went down to the Cornerstone Grill and began to drink like I always did when I went out.

I was standing at the bar and there was a woman with her back turned toward me talking to some of her friends. I touched her waist to get her attention and to see if she wanted to dance. From that point, things spiraled out of control. Although I won't go into detail, and I may never be able to tell my full side, I will say that it was never my intention to hurt or harm anyone. My intention was to try to dance and socialize, but I know now that it is not always the intention of your actions that matters but the impact that they have.

I left the bar immediately and went home. I took the incident as a sign that I needed to stay away from the bar scene and keep my focus on basketball. The season was about to start and I needed to use my last season at Maryland to make an impression if I wanted to make it to the NBA.

The season started off with the Maui Invitational in Hawaii. I played well, but not great. The word was that some NBA teams were talking about me because I played well in Maui. We had lost to Gonzaga in a tough game, but then went on to win our next two games. Even with the wins, I still wasn't performing to everyone's expectations, or even my own. People were beginning to give up on me. Others were like, "After four years, Garrison, give us something."

The pressure had me thinking too much again. The confidence is not there whenever I begin to think too much about each shot and what teammates, coaches, fans, and sports writers are thinking about me. My self-doubts were back and standing up like the guy in the Madison Square Garden screaming, "Travis Garrison, you suck!"

After Maui, things had pretty much been the usual up and down play for me. Good one night, disappear the next. When we went to Duke and lost, I felt like I needed to do something as a senior leader. I wrote a four page letter to the team. The coaching staff made copies for me and distributed it to the team. The letter seemed to make a mild impact but was soon overshadowed by the firestorm about to erupt.

When I came out of class on Friday, January 13, 2006, I received a call from an assistant coach whose words sent fear through me, "Travis, you have to turn yourself into the Hyattsville police."

After I turned myself in for booking and fingerprinting, I was free to go. I was upset, but thought that nobody else would have known besides the officers, the young lady involved, and the coaching staff. From the police station, I went into the locker room. Within 10 minutes, I was told that the story was running all over the news. As soon as I left the Comcast Center, my phone was ringing non-stop. I had my girlfriend come pick me up, and we went to get something to eat just so I could get away. I turned my phone off because I was getting bombarded with phone calls and messages and I was starting to feel stressed. I hadn't even begun to process the implications of my arrest and what it could mean for my future.

By the time I had finished eating, which took about 45 minutes or so, I turned my phone back on and saw that I had over forty messages. That fast, I felt like the situation was getting crazy and overwhelming. I just needed some type of comfort. So I did something I had gotten away from doing since I started college. I picked up my Bible and started reading. I had not read the Bible in a long time and now I couldn't stop reading it. I called an elder from my church and he talked with me for a long time. He was very understanding and loving, but it was tough love. He was brutally honest with me. He told me that I had become like luke-warm water and I made God sick and he had vomited me out of his mouth that night in October.

The elder was clear that God still loved me, but that I needed to start living right. I had to change—really change this time, no games. Although it was tough to hear, I knew he was right. Sometimes people, even our closest friends, will tell you what they think you want to hear instead of telling you what you need to hear. It is always good to have people in your corner who will tell you the truth, no matter what.

There was another person I wanted to talk to that weekend, but couldn't. My grandmother had passed away right before the basketball banquet following my junior year and close to my brother L's 30th birthday. She was always so positive. Her absence was kind of a double-edged sword. While I really wanted to talk to her, I was glad she did not hear the terrible things being said about me in the press.

Throughout this book, I have been careful not to make any excuses for the negative things that happened to me. The same is true here; I take full responsibility for this nightmare. It doesn't even matter that I never really got the chance to tell my side. I should not have been in the bar in the first place. I put myself in a position where a stranger had the power to change my life.

I had broken my own commitment to myself and lost the chance to realize my full potential that year and have a season so great that I would be drafted by the NBA. Now basketball was the least of my problems. The story in the Washington Post sports section the day after my arrest said:

> Garrison, who practiced yesterday following his appearance before Prince George's police, faces up to 10 years in prison and a $2,500 fine for the assault charge. For the sex offense, he faces up to one year in prison and a $1,000 fine.

My court date was set for June, so after serving my one game suspension, just like the football players received, I was allowed to rejoin the team. I played, but Coach Williams never started me again until Senior Night, which was our last regular season home game. Gary and I had bumped heads a number of times during my career at Maryland. He wanted me to be a better post player and I felt more comfortable facing the basket, but even when we were at odds, he had never given up on me. Not until my arrest, then it all changed.

I played poorly on Senior Night and we went into the ACC Tournament as the sixth seed. We beat Georgia Tech in the first game and then lost to Boston College in the second round. We were losing big in that game and I took an open shot and missed. During the next time-out, Gary really ripped into me. Anyone who has seen Gary coach won't be surprised to hear that he would make his displeasure known to the players, but this time, it was obviously personal.

Everyone sitting in the stands behind the bench heard what Gary was saying to me and I felt my body flood with anger. When we went to the team dinner after the game, I was ready to snap. I was waiting for Gary to say something to me, but he never did and I am grateful for that. With us both being so angry, nothing good could've come from another confrontation.

Looking back now, I can understand why Coach was so disappointed. I had disappointed myself during my time at Maryland, but that was not all. This senior class was supposed to be something special. Gary brought us to Maryland as the first recruiting class after the Terps won the National Championship. Everyone expected big things from us and we expected them from ourselves. It must have hurt Coach to think that of the four players recruited in that class, three of us had been arrested on various charges during our careers.

My career at Maryland ended with a loss to Manhattan in the first round of the NIT. I was playing for my future and finished the game with 21 points and 12 rebounds. We were the number one seed in the tournament and lost 87-84 to the number 36 seed in a field of 40 teams that did not make the NCAA Tournament. These excerpts about the game from the ESPN story online are not the way the "fearsome foursome," wanted to be remembered:

> If the result of the game hinged solely on talent, Manhattan probably wouldn't have stood a chance.... The Jaspers were far more inspired than the Terrapins, however....
>
> Instead of sulking, Manhattan decided to make up for the disappointment of missing the NCAA Tournament with an inspired performance.
>
> Angered over being left out of the NCAA Tournament, the Terrapins (19-13) initially declined the NIT bid late Sunday night. But coach Gary Williams reversed the decision after speaking with the NIT committee chairman C.M. Newton.
>
> The disappointment, however, lingered.

That last line pretty much sums up my career at Maryland and the "can't miss" kid dropped out of school during spring break.

FOULS AND FREE THROWS

Play hard, learn from your mistakes, then MOVE ON!

Players: I may not have lived up to expectations on the court, but I lived up to them off the court. People expected to see me in the bars and they did! I have mentioned partying and going to clubs a number of times and I want to speak directly to that whole scene now and to how we handle our mistakes in life and on the court.

Partying for me was about being liked. I wanted people to see me and say, "Hey, that's Travis Garrison," and then see how approachable and friendly I was even with strangers. Unfortunately, I also drank too much when I went out. Luckily that would one day change my life. You have to make good choices in your life. If you keep pushing your luck, some day you are going lose and lose big. TRUST ME, it's not worth it.

You already know that even as a little boy I always wanted people to like me. That is true to this day even though I have learned not to take negative criticism personally. If it's hard for you to take the criticism from fans or sports writers online, in the papers, or on radio and TV, then don't read, watch, or listen to them! If reading that stuff motivates you to do better, then eat it all up! Everyone is different, just know yourself and do what is best for you.

Trying to live life without making mistakes is like trying to play basketball without ever committing a foul. If you are always worried about fouling, you won't play very well. You can't dominate with your mind on a negative thought like "I'm not going to foul." Play hard and work hard and live hard and you will sometimes make mistakes. The question is really, when you make a mistake, how do you handle it? Do you ignore it and pretend it didn't happen? Do you deny it to yourself and others? Does every little mistake eat at you and keep you awake at night and distract you on the court? Or do you face your mistakes and obstacles head on and learn from them and move on? TRUST ME, if I had learned to handle life the last way, things might have been different.

A man once told me, "Have the mind of a defensive back. Once the play is over, forget it. You do not have time to focus on the mistake you made the previous play because it's on to the next down and you have to focus on that one." After the game, study your mistakes on film or just review them in your mind so that you do not repeat them, then move on. The same thing goes off the court when you make mistakes. Own up to them, face them head on, learn from them, and then get on with your life.

No matter what things may be going on at the time, they will get better as long as you do not keep going over and over the mistakes and your bad games. Learn from them and get on with it. Use those bad times to motivate yourself. Go into the gym and work even harder. Don't let those same mistakes happen again. There is a great line in the movie "Shawshank Redemption" that comes when a falsely imprisoned man is discouraged after twenty years. A friend tells him, "You got two choices, you can get busy livin' or you can get busy dyin'."

Play hard, learn from your mistakes, then MOVE ON!

7

Starting Over

NBA Dreams

After dropping out of school, I started training with Keith Williams, who had trained a lot of NBA players. I was preparing myself for the NBA draft. During that time, the first pre-draft NBA camp in Portsmouth, Virginia came up. I reached out to Coach Wootten who put me in touch with the director of the camp. I had called and requested to be given a spot, but he told me they were full, but encouraged me to call back in a couple days and see if anything changed.

By this time I started to get discouraged because I saw this camp as the first real opportunity to get my name back on the map. I called him back a few days later, only to be told that they were still full, but he thanked me for being so eager to join the camp. I thanked him for his time. I thought I had missed another opportunity, but a few minutes later he called me back and said that another player had gotten hurt and I could take his spot. I was so excited and thankful. I really wanted to make a good impression. The camp was a lot like the ABCD camp where I came in as the underdog among players who were getting a lot more attention.

I was still battling the reputation I got at Maryland for disappearing during games, but I was focused and ready both physically and mentally. I averaged 13 points, nine rebounds a game during camp. I was swamped by agents. After each game, a lot of agents would approach the players, looking to sign us as clients. It felt great, but I was really not prepared to make a good decision about which agent would be best for me at that time, especially being in the position I was in.

I had made a pretty good impression at the camp. After the last game, I was approached by an agent who was a former Terp. He asked to represent me, and I agreed. I was excited by the plans he had for me and by the impact I made at the camp. I was an honorable mention on the All-tournament team. One draft expert said that I had a good chance of being a late second-round pick.

After the camp in Portsmouth, my agent made plans for me to attend IMG in Florida. IMG is a state-of-the-art training facility for a variety of sports. A lot of projected top draft picks train there before working out with teams and the NBA draft camp in Chicago. I got a chance to showcase my skills with all the top picks. It felt good and draft writers were saying that my stock was going up. The plan was to generate enough interest to have teams invite me to work out for them. I already had an agent, but another agent gave me some friendly advice by coming up with a list of teams that had needs that I might be able to fill. That was the kind of agent I needed, but at the time I didn't feel like I should make a change.

I only got one invite to workout. Danny Ferry, the general manager of the Cleveland Cavaliers gave me an opportunity. Danny's father was the long-time GM of the Washington Bullets (now the Wizards) and Danny is a DeMatha graduate who went on to have a great career at Duke and a long career in the NBA. I knew the DeMatha brotherhood connection made me appealing to Danny, but he had a job to do and I had to perform if I expected to be signed by him.

I showed up for my workout in a suit with my workout gear in my bag. I wanted to be as professional as possible and do things right. I was grateful for the opportunity and I made sure Danny knew how grateful I was for his help. Before the workout I had some time to talk to his father Bob Ferry and he told me that he thought I would be a good fit, but that rebounding was a concern. My workout was good, but not great, and I did not hear anything back from Cleveland.

My agent couldn't get me into the NBA pre-draft camp in Chicago, which made me very upset. That was an important camp. All the top prospects were going to be there and I wasn't. I kept hearing that lots of teams were talking about me, but the Cleveland workout was the only one I got before the draft.

Just four years before, I was graduating from DeMatha and was on top of the world. Not only did I expect to have an NBA career, but I was sure that I would come out of Maryland early, certainly as a junior or maybe even as a sophomore. Now I couldn't even get into the most important pre-draft NBA camp, had only one workout with Cleveland, and no other direct contact with any teams.

My court date came up two days before the draft. The timing could not have been worse. I naively thought that just getting it over with was the best option. The prosecutors were pushing me for a plea bargain and threatening me with having to register as a sex offender.

If the case went to court and I lost, I would face potential jail time and be labeled as a sex offender for the rest of my life. In order to avoid that, I pled guilty to sexual assault. Next to actually going to the bar that night, that guilty plea was the biggest mistake of my life. Even in terms of the impact on my draft standing or possible free agent signing, it would have been better to plead not guilty and have a new court date set for the trial. That would have kept the story out of the papers until after the draft and buy time to better understand my case. There were so many times in my life that I was not prepared to handle the non-basketball challenges that I faced.

Draft day came and went and I was not drafted. What should have been the happiest day of my life up to that point was lonely and disappointing. I had always imagined a big draft day party or even being invited to New York as one of the projected top picks. I knew my friends and family were all thinking about what could have been, what should have been.

I will never know if draft day would have turned out differently if we were not living in the age of the internet. Everything about our lives that is available to the public, and even some that is supposed to be private, can be found by anyone with a computer and internet access. I can only assume that when teams began to do research on me, the headline, "Terrapins' Garrison Is Charged with Assault and

Sex Offense" came up, and that was it. They weren't going to take a chance on someone with that history and a subpar college career. There is a good chance that it will be on the first page of search results for the rest of my life.

After the draft, I attempted to land a spot on an NBA summer league team. When that didn't happen, I went to the next best thing, which was a summer league team that played games before and after the NBA summer league games. That way, NBA scouts and coaches would still be able to see me play. I went to LA to play in the pro summer league where I was playing against guys who were all looking to get picked up by an NBA team. I was playing with a chip on my shoulder at this point. I should not have been in this situation and it was my own fault. While in LA, Laron Profit, a fellow Terrapin playing for the Lakers, took me under his wing. We worked out together and he gave me a lot of advice on what it meant to be a professional basketball player. I played well and was offered $80,000 to play in France and six figures to play in Japan. That was a lot of money compared to what I was making, but my agent said to keep my eye on the NBA.

When the summer league ended, I came back home and was playing and working out hard. I was really tempted when I received another six-figure offer to play in Europe. I was working out with my good friend Corey McCrae, and told him I had decided to take the offer. I planned to pursue the NBA the following season. After our workout, I called my agent to let him know my decision. He agreed, but a few minutes later called me back to let me know that the LA Lakers were showing a strong interest. We decided to hold off on the offer in Europe and continue to pursue my chances with the Lakers.

It turned out that the Lakers didn't bring me on as a free agent, but selected me in the seventh round of the D-League draft. The D-League is the NBA's Developmental League, which is a minor league for the NBA. It might sound funny, but it felt good to be wanted by anyone associated with the NBA. Remember, even as a little boy, I wanted to be liked; now as a young man, it felt good to be wanted. During the draft, the commentator projected me to be the first player called up to the NBA.

The only problem with playing basketball for the Lakers' organization was that I had to learn the triangle offense. Right at the most critical time in my quest to play in the NBA, I couldn't just play free flowing instinctive basketball. Thinking was the LAST thing I needed to be doing on the court!

The triangle offense is extremely complicated and takes a long time to learn. It involves a lot of details that are difficult to remember. We were being taught by Tex Winter, one of the early developers of the system. Phil Jackson won eleven NBA titles running the triangle offense. It looks smooth when you know what you are doing, but when you don't, it looks pretty ugly.

I worked hard to make the team. I watched each guy get cut with a sense of relief and hope. It came down to one more cut and I was feeling pretty confident. When they released me, my teammates thought it had to be a joke. It wasn't a joke and I was shocked. I just knew that this was my chance, and just like the commentator at the draft said, I would be one of the first ones called up to the NBA.

I headed home and started working out again, despite being heavily disappointed by what happened in LA. While at home, I met Vanessa, who would one day become my wife. We spent a lot of time together until I got an offer from a CBA team. The CBA is the Continental Basketball Association. It is a professional league and a lot of former NBA players and NBA hopefuls play in it. So, just before Christmas, I headed out to Great Falls, Montana. I left with determination. If I was going to get to realize my dream of playing in the NBA, I had to be a great player in the CBA first.

FOULS AND FREE THROWS

Be prepared for the next move on and off the court!

Parents: If your child has the talent and has worked hard enough to be receiving college scholarship offers, you need to be prepared to help in the selection process. After that, if your child is considered professional material, you need to make sure he or she knows how to choose a good agent. After high school, basketball is a business and players need to be educated about the business of sports, not just how to play the game on the court.

Players: College is a business, where you are getting paid with a free education. It is foolish not to take advantage of the educational opportunity no matter how good of a player you are or think you are. I know like me, some players go into college with the mindset that they are going to the pros and education is not important. That is FALSE. You NEVER know what can happen. Even if things work out for you and you go to the next level, as long as you are in college, it is smart to do your best.

As hard as it is to hear, your athletic career will be taken from you one day. You might not be as good as you think or, God forbid, you get severely injured. Even the greatest players in the world have it taken away by getting older. Education is one thing someone can NEVER take from you. The reality is that a very low percentage of players make it to the NBA, NFL, etc. If that is your dream, you should strive towards it. Just make sure you are taking advantage of the educational opportunities generated from your athletic ability.

Maybe you think that you can be a coach and make the kind of money professional and college coaches make. Do you think they are hiring dummies who did not take college seriously? Most coaching positions require a college degree, including a high school coaching position.

It doesn't matter what your resume was BEFORE getting to college; what matters is how you perform while you are there. Yes, you may have a name walking onto campus, but it's what you do to keep that name that matters. Are you working out the same as you were to get that name? You want to make it professionally, but are you working out and staying focus on getting there? Are you partying more than working out? Are you focused more on what you are doing AFTER practice, rather than what's going IN practice? How bad do you want it? Are you still living off what you did in high school? If the answer is yes, then let me just tell you that you are in trouble.

Another thing to watch out for are the critics, tune them out as best you can. You may get praised and treated like a king if you have a good game, but have a bad one and look out. They will rip you to shreds. You have to be strong-minded, and not focus on what people are saying and blogging about you. Just focus on being the best you can be. Give yourself a fair chance; maximize your potential and see how good you can really be.

Do not cheat yourself. Consider all of that hard work you put in to get there. Do not let it go to waste for a few hours of fun. Are all those long hours in the gym, all those suicides, extra shots, weight lifting just to get recruited or do you want more? If you REALLY want to make it, then you MUST sacrifice. TRUST ME, all the partying and the girls and alcohol will be your downfall.

It's the coach's job to bring players in who they think can help them win and if you are not doing that, then they will definitely find someone who will. It's nothing personal, it's a business. Have people around you who will let you know when you are doing wrong, not those who are just along for the ride.

There will be a lot of people who just want to be around you because of who you are and what they can get from you. Those are the people that will NOT be there if you do not make it, TRUST ME. Stay focused, have that same mindset and attitude you had entering college and you will reach your dream. If not, then at least you gave yourself the best possible chance to do so. Do not cheat yourself or your talents; it is your gift from God. Take care of that gift, develop it or the opportunity will go to someone who might even be less talented than you but did things right and appreciates it more.

When it comes to picking an agent, don't necessarily go with an agent because of who they are or because someone tells you that you should go with them. Do your research. Get with an agent that you feel comfortable with, one who you know has your best interest at heart. You also want an agent who has experience. The agent you pick is speaking on behalf of you. You want to make sure that person is working their hardest for you. Sometimes going with that big name agent means you may get lost in the shuffle because that agent has too many clients and may not be able to show you the attention you deserve, want, and need. On the other hand, a smaller agency might not have as many connections or leverage. Again, the important thing is to do your research. Most importantly, don't forget the agent works for you, not the other way around.

8

Reputation and Consequences

The CBA and Around the World

Here I was, a city guy in Great Falls, Montana and I loved it! I missed Vanessa, but other than that, the CBA was one of the best times of my life. We played Utah in the first game and I scored over 20 points. It was a great way to start. The bus travel was brutal, but everyone was friendly and we all got along well. I loved the coaching staff; they were good and they let me play my game.

Bus travel was a big step down from my days at Maryland where we flew to more than a dozen games a year on chartered flights and had all of our meals provided. We didn't even have a per diem when I was in the CBA. Because of all the bus travel, we played back-to-back games in the same city.

It is easy to become a basketball snob and think that the good players are only in the major colleges and the NBA. I found out that is not true. Everywhere I have played, I have met outstanding players and the CBA was no exception. It only makes sense that if I considered myself a good player, then the CBA must have some good players because I am one of them.

I was paid $600 a week, which was a far cry from even the $80,000 I was offered during the summer to play in France. Despite the low pay, I still felt that the CBA was the best place for me to be noticed by the NBA. The veterans on the team definitely treated me like the rookie that I was. I had to carry the their bags and things like that. The people of Montana were amazing. They treated us great.

The inevitable head bumping with the coaches happened even though I really liked them. I couldn't quite figure out how I could score 25 points one game and then only play five minutes in the next. Even so, I was named CBA Rookie of the Year. I was a professional for the first time in my life and it felt good.

The CBA has quality players and coaches and I was able to learn the ropes from the veterans. Vanessa made it out to some games, which really helped me handle being away from home. There was also a married couple that had me in their home. It was nice to get some home cooked meals and just to be around a family environment.

2006-07 GREAT FALLS EXPLORERS

I went home after the season and felt good about my first professional experience. Talking to the veterans helped me change my opinion about playing overseas and I learned that getting good game film was the way to get picked up internationally. I was ready to take the next step in my career, but I still had a lot of maturing to do.

During the offseason, I made a decision that I felt was best for me at the time. I fired my agent and signed with the agent who had originally shown me that list of teams that I should have been contacting right after I did so well in the Portsmouth camp.

Right off the bat he got me a workout with the 76ers. I had a pretty good workout. Afterwards, I met with the head coach, Maurice Cheeks, and the GM, Billy King. Billy King asked me what I thought I needed to work on and I told them the truth—my post game and defense. Then I turned the question around and asked them what they thought I should work on. I wanted to let them know I was coachable and ready to work hard.

I got a second workout for Cleveland with Danny Ferry. I felt ready when I went to Cleveland and played in three tryout games. This time I got a chance to talk with Danny Ferry as well as his dad, Bob Ferry. I was very careful to express how thankful I was to be given this opportunity. Everyone always had kind and encouraging words, but it always ended with something like, "Keep up the good work". It never resulted in an NBA contract.

By the summer of 2007, Vanessa and I had gotten pretty serious. She is an amazing person and really has a deep commitment to her faith. I have learned so much from her and I know her prayers have kept me going many times. But things just weren't happening for me professionally and so she suggested we do a 40-day progressive fast. The way it worked was that we would give up a few things each week until the last week when we couldn't eat anything except fruits and vegetables. So I started out with giving up drinking.

I was tempted a lot during those 40 days. I guess that's the idea, to just keep depending on God. The daily gratitude list really helped. Every day Vanessa and I would each write down one thing for which we were grateful. It is easy to forget how blessed you are until you stop and count your blessings. That helped me realize that even though I was not playing in the NBA, I had a whole lot to be thankful for in my life.

What seemed like an answer to our prayers came during the fast. I was offered $180,000 to play in Japan. My agent had the contract and we were ready to sign when the Japanese team called and backed out. The team owner had done an internet search and you know what came up. I was still paying for that one bad decision to go to the bar that night in 2005. This time the payment was $180,000.

It was kind of hard to believe on the one hand, but it isn't surprising after what happened with the Lakers. Teams only know what they read, they don't really know me. They are also concerned about the bad PR if their fans find out about it, which they will. The Japanese culture is very sensitive to bringing in Americans so anything like my assault conviction is a red flag. All this was my fault, not theirs; they were just looking out for their own best interest.

I was crushed. It is tempting to blame God when you fast and pray and then it seems like you have an answer to your prayers only to have the rug pulled out from under you. I went to Bishop Larry Jordan, the pastor at the Believer's Worship Center, my church at the time. He had a simple, but hopeful answer for me: "When God closes a door, he opens a window."

At least now, I had an agent who was always on top of things. Soon after the Japanese disappointment, he called and said that there was a South Korean camp in Las Vegas that I should attend. The South Korean professional teams would all have scouts and coaches there and hold a draft right after the camp.

I attended the camp and I played great. All the Koreans were calling me Jordan, as in Michael Jordan, because of how I was scoring and dunking. I got drafted in the second round by the SK Knights. When I signed the contract, the GM handed me an envelope with $10,000 cash in it! I called Vanessa and gave her the good news. She had been supporting me for so long and it felt good to be carrying my share now.

The good news was that I had $10,000 in my pocket; the bad news was that I was in Las Vegas! That night I took full advantage of the Las Vegas nightlife. I hung out with John Smith, the other American player drafted by the SK Knights. We hit up casinos and nightclubs until the early morning, spending some of our $10,000 advance.

When I got back to DC, I spent more money, but this time it was spent on more worthwhile expenses. I gave my mom some money because she had always worked so hard to provide for us. Then I took my whole family out to eat at a pretty expensive restaurant. God has blessed me with a large extended family. That was my way of saying thank you to everyone for all the years of support and for believing in me.

I left for Korea in August. Everything there was first class including the plane flight over. We got a huge welcome. The team facilities had everything including saunas, weight room, beautiful apartments, and flat screen TVs. Whatever you wanted or needed, they made sure you got it.

The other side of that coin was the brutal practices and the almost impossible expectations of the American players, including me. Each team was allowed to have two American players. In the first and second quarters, only one of us was allowed on the court at a time. In the second half, both of us could play at the same time.

Unlike what I would experience playing in other countries, the South Koreans gave us a team translator. One of the things we had him translate was about the practices. We told him to tell the coaches that if they didn't ease up, it would hurt our performances. It was just too much, but they did not ease up and it really did hurt how we played.

They flew us to Portland, Oregon and we worked out at the Blazers' facilities. We played against some NBA players there. Vanessa came to visit before we went back to Korea. I was to tell her about the experience so far and how crazy it was at times; but it was good money so I had to see it through.

It got to be just like Maryland as far as the coaches demanded post play from me. I felt that whole trauma coming back. Even when I scored 40 points, the head coach got on me for "how" I scored them. I didn't need the translator to tell me the meaning of the words when I was being chewed out. Here I was again, butting heads with my coaches. I had to wonder if it was me; I always seemed to be at odds with the coaches wherever I played since leaving DeMatha.

The coaches were very aggressive toward me, but did not treat John Smith that way. I assumed it was because I was so young compared to everyone else. I'm glad John caught a break, but I was not having fun again. When I say not having fun, I am not saying that because the practices were hard. I have always worked hard and still had fun. The satisfaction of working hard is part of the fun.

It was not fun because of the way I was being treated. The coaches were feeling pressure from the owner and then putting that pressure on me, but the fans loved me. Everyone was calling me Moon Tae Jr. who was a great Korean basketball star. He was a great shooter. I loved that everyone expected me to be the man, but I had to be the man with my game and not having every move criticized.

We started the season with a winning record. We were very isolated where we lived and trained, but our home games were in Seoul, the capital of South Korea. We were rock stars as soon as we got off the buses in Seoul and my name was chanted by the whole arena during games: GAR-I-SON, GAR-I-SON! Shavery was able to come over to see me play. I'm glad he got to hear the chanting, which was very cool for him. Whenever we went into Seoul to play, we got the next day off in the city. They would put us up in a hotel room and then later in the evening I would head out to a club.

It was one thing to put up with being mistreated when we were winning, but then we began to lose. The pressure grew and so did the trash talking, which motivated me at first, but then I began to go into some dark places inside myself. I had been there before and did not want to go there again. I began to shut down. One night, after a bad game, I called my agent and naively told him to find me somewhere else for the same money. When I went to the club that night to have some fun, I heard a rumor that I had been replaced.

The next day the GM called me in to have lunch with him. He liked me a lot and my problems were never with him. The lunch meeting was very emotional. He told me that I was being released. On one hand, I felt some relief. It was obvious I wasn't happy. On the other hand, I felt some disappointment. The fans loved me and I was playing well. My manager explained to me that they wanted to bring in someone with more experience.

I had to stay around a while before I could arrange to get back home so I even went to the team banquet that evening. Even though we were parting ways, I still had become quite close with some of my teammates and didn't want to end on bad terms.

At least I had some money now and, when I got back home, I began to spend it. I bought tables at the club and bought things for my family. I traded in my Lexus for a Benz with a $900 monthly payment. I loved to do things to surprise my family. It wasn't that I was doing bad things with my money, but a lot of money was going out and nothing was coming in.

During this time, Vanessa took custody of her half-brother, Jonas. Jonas was only two-years-old and his parents could no longer care for him. After much discussion, we decided that we did not want to see him in foster care, and he came to live with her in DC. Having no children of our own yet, we became instant parents.

I was home for about three weeks before heading to the second division league in Spain with a one-month contract. This was a great league, very highly respected. The team did not provide a translator and I began to regret not paying attention in Spanish class at DeMatha. I played well, but did not get many minutes. We only played once a week, but I was not happy. I was not getting along with a few of my teammates and I was tempted to leave. But I needed the exposure that this league could give me if I wanted to get to the NBA. So, I decided to stay and hope for a contract extension.

In January, my brother L was getting married. I told the coach I needed to go home for his wedding. We had four days off around that time, so I assumed it wouldn't be much of an issue. The coach said that I could only go if we win the next game. I didn't like it, but I agreed. We won, but the coach said I still could not go because the GM of the team wanted to meet with me. I was very upset because it was really important to be me to be at his wedding. I decided to go without the team's permission. There was a rumor that I was going to be cut, and I foolishly assumed that is what the GM wanted to talk to me about.

Now some might think I made the right move. It was my brother's wedding and the coach did go back on his word. But I acted out of emotion and not rational thinking. As a professional, I hadn't yet learned the importance of putting emotions to the side to make the best business decision. I found out through my agent that the team was prepared to extend my contract, but felt like I had acted unprofessionally when I left, and never made the offer. My immature attitude was "whatever," but little did I know that the decision to leave Spain would have a ripple effect.

When I got another offer right away from Qatar in the Middle East, it looked like I had landed on my feet again. I flew to Qatar and practiced with the team before I signed the contract. I liked the coaches and the practices were easy. I still had to get a physical exam before signing.

I was there for about a week before learning that the team in Spain still owned my rights, which means I was still under contract with them. They refused to release me until I paid back half of the money they had paid me. I paid back the money but due to some other issues with the contract in Qatar, I decided it wasn't the right situation and I left.

Now I was getting a reputation. The basketball world is a small one. Coaches talk to coaches and GM's talk to GM's. I was bouncing around from place to place, which wasn't good. Teams wanted to know why I was leaving early.

A few weeks after I left Qatar, I received an offer to play in Venezuela. One of my teammates, Reuben, immediately became like a big brother to me. I was making good money and was having fun with basketball again. When Reuben got hurt, my playing time increased and I was doing really well, but the coach faced pressure from the owners to make sure the domestic players were getting their playing time, so my playing time was cut.

I was only in Venezuela a few weeks when my grandfather died. I told the team that I wanted to go home for the funeral. Unlike what happened in Spain, the team agreed and even paid for my ticket. I left all my things in Venezuela and went home for the funeral. When I was ready to return, I looked at my ticket and realized it was one way. I tried to contact the team, but no one would answer my calls or emails. It was almost two months before the team finally brought me back to help them make it to the playoffs. Because they had so many domestic players who played my position, they hesitated to bring me back to allow them to get their share of playing time. We eventually ended up in third place for the season.

That summer, Vanessa and I were married and went on our honeymoon to the Dominican Republic. Upon our return, I got an offer from Argentina to play for $90,000. I was recovering from a herniated abdominal muscle and was not able to report on time. I lost the contract and started looking for another team. When I was fully recovered, I was contacted by the top team in Uruguay. They paid for my flight there to sign a contract and begin playing immediately.

At this point, all the money I had made in the previous season was gone. Being foolish, I had spent more money than I had coming in. Vanessa was teaching elementary school, and we were able to get by on her salary, but very little was left at the end of each month. I had to fly to South America without a dime to my name, but happy that I would soon be making some money again.

This was only my second year playing overseas, and my third as a professional, so I still had my sights set on the NBA. As soon as I got to Uruguay, I got a call to play in Turkey. It was second division, but Turkey is a strong basketball country and I knew I would get a lot more exposure being in Europe. It was a tough decision, but I told the Uruguay team that I was not signing with them. Not surprisingly, they refused to pay for my hotel expenses. Because I didn't have any money, I couldn't pay and they threatened to arrest me. Once again, I was contributing to my reputation of being unprofessional and unreliable. My agent was like, "Travis, you went to another country with no money in your pocket?!"

I finally got everything straightened out and got a flight to Denizli, Turkey. One of the most embarrassing moments of my life was arriving in Turkey and not having $20 to pay for my VISA. I had to ask a complete stranger for the money.

Despite the hardship of getting out of Uruguay, playing in Turkey turned out to be a good move. I had great teammates and the coach treated me like a son. The team even flew Vanessa and Jonas over, and they stayed for most of the season. The fans were terrific and I was playing well. I averaged better than 20 points and 10 rebounds a game. I was named to first team all-league and first team all-defensive team, which really made me happy.

Now that I was playing at the top of my game, the question that kept coming up was, "What happened at Maryland?" People who hadn't heard of me before or did not follow me at Maryland would search my name on the internet and wonder how I could have struggled so much in college. Why wasn't I in the NBA?

As much as I enjoyed my first season in Turkey, it was still only second division and I needed to move up to keep pursuing my dream. I went back home and waited for a call. Vanessa had become pregnant while we were it Turkey and it was good that I was there. She had a very normal pregnancy until she was about 38 weeks, then one day she noticed the baby had stopped moving.

    I took her to the emergency room and they could not find the baby's heartbeat. The symptoms probably meant that the placenta had ruptured. There was significant internal bleeding and we weren't sure how long the baby had gone without the blood from the placenta that was giving him his oxygen. Vanessa was rushed into the operating room for an emergency C-section. Travis Jr., our son, did not have a detectable heartbeat or breathe for the first 17 minutes of his life, but thankfully, he was revived. Both he and Vanessa almost died, but both made full recoveries. It was one of the scariest times of my life, but it was a reminder of the daily gratitude list we used to make during that fast. I was and am truly blessed.

    During the offseason, my only offer was to go back to the same team in second division in Turkey. I didn't want to go back to second division but it was my best option at the time. At the start of the season, I was dominating and leading the league in scoring, but we were losing. There are a lot of lessons athletes learn from sports whether their teams win or lose. However, winning is the objective of every game and when you are a professional, winning is really the only thing that matters.

    So, in spite of my great play, I was not happy. I am not just about individual accomplishment. The same coach who had treated me like a son the year before was feeling the stress of losing and it hurt our relationship. I was looking forward to going home for the Christmas holidays. When I got home, I found out how tough things were on Vanessa. She was carrying all of the weight of being a single parent. On top of the fact that I was not happy playing second division ball in Turkey, I had not been able to spend any significant time with TJ since his birth. I had left for Turkey only two weeks after his traumatic birth. So, I decided not to go back to Denizli. That was just another unprofessional move on my part and added to my reputation of not being loyal to the organizations that hired me. I knew this, but felt strongly that it was something I needed to do, for myself and my family.

After being home for about a month, I changed agents again and signed to play in Ukraine on a Euro Challenge team. My agent and I decided it was best for me to play on that team because it was a higher level of basketball and could lead to a good situation for the following year.

I did not know what to expect in the Ukraine. The only thing I knew about the country was that it is SUPER cold there. I was anxious to start playing again, but getting there was a challenge. There was a bad snowstorm in the DC area and the airports were closed. One thing about some basketball clubs overseas is that when they want you there they want you there as soon as possible, especially if it's already in the middle of the season. Unfortunately, my flight was cancelled three different times, and the club was getting frustrated and impatient. I just wanted to get there and not lose my spot because this situation was exactly what I needed to get my career back on course.

This was a new team, a new country, another language to pick up on, and a whole other culture to learn. When I arrived, I got to know my teammates and they were cool. I met the coach and he was young and seemed laid back, so I felt like this was another coach who may be good for me. He liked my game, but the team was trying to make the playoffs and needed to make some changes and that was one of the reasons I was brought in.

A few days after being there and playing well, they fired the coach. I was in a situation where I needed to do what I had to do to make an impression and to also solidify my job for the next season. Now suddenly I had a new coach. He was an older guy and didn't know my game except for what the assistant coach told him.

After the new head coach came, I wasn't getting as much playing time as before. They brought in two more players, one in my position. I was told he was not coming for my spot, but he was only coming in to help us make the playoffs. There was only a month left in the regular season and it didn't really look like we were going to make the playoffs.

I started playing more the last three games of the regular season and was averaging 17 points and seven rebounds. We ended up not making the playoffs and they released all the Americans except me and the point guard.

We had to play in the "play-outs," which was for teams to see which teams would finish 9-14th place. This was the first time I heard of this, and I really just wanted to get back home because I missed my family. The American point guard received an offer from another team in another country to help them in their playoff run, so I was the only American left. I thought there was going to be a lot of pressure by me being the only American, but I ended up playing really well in the play-outs. I averaged about 12 points and seven rebounds a game.

Once the season ended, I thought, "I'm back! I should get some great offers after all this." I played in a solid league and proved I can play at that level. I knew I could do it, but other teams might have questioned it. The summer came, and I was excited about what offers I might receive. As time went on, it became yet another summer where things were not happening like I thought they would.

Despite being disappointed with the lack of offers, I knew I had to keep pushing. Now I'm both a husband and a father and I have responsibilities. Now I'm not doing this just for the love of the game, but to be able to provide for my family.

I ended up going back to the same team in Ukraine, a place I thought I would never go back to. I was told it would be a good situation because of the Euro Challenge, which meant we would be able to play against different countries and get more exposure. Even though Ukraine was not my top choice, I told myself that I had to do what I had to do.

It was a different coach now, which was one of the main reasons I didn't mind going back. The coach was real cool; he was Croatian, more of a player's coach. He demanded a lot, but he could also be laid back. He definitely liked to have fun, a LOT of fun! I signed a two-month deal because the coach really didn't know a lot about me and wanted to make sure that he liked me. One thing I didn't mind was being on a tryout basis.

I knew I would go in and get the spot, especially if I was determined. I won the position, but I started slow and couldn't find my rhythm mostly because of my workout schedule that summer. I wasn't able to train like I wanted to because of watching my son all day and being exhausted by the evening. It was really difficult to make my work outs a priority. So, the first few games we played were games against a team from Romania, which we had to beat to qualify for Euro Challenge.

We ended up beating them and qualifying. After that they fired our coach. I guess because the domestic players didn't like him. He would get on them, but I always felt he had good intentions when doing so. However, the other players didn't like it, so they had him fired. That just goes to show you that some places are cut throat. Even though it's overseas ball and not the NBA it's just as tough; especially to make it the whole season.

They made our assistant coach the head coach for a little while and he let me play my game to an extent. I was coming up on the last month of my two-month contract. There was an assistant coach who was a young guy and really cool. He was easy to get along with and worked with me after practice on different game moves and getting up a lot of shots.

Doing that helped me. I started to get that swag in my game again. I was getting to the place where I knew no one could stop me and I started playing like it. Attitude is everything. I was helping my team win games, and scoring big numbers. This was mainly because of the work I had been putting in AFTER practice, and that EXTRA work that really makes the difference. Now it started to show in my game and just at the right time for my contract to be up.

About a week into the last month of my contract, we got ANOTHER coach. I didn't know what to expect and the day after we had a tough game we had a hard practice. I was thinking to myself, "Oh boy, this is going to be crazy." He didn't believe in taking days off as much, but the first game he had coached just so happened to be one of the best games in my whole career against one of the top teams in our league and in Europe. I had close to 25 points. It would have won us the game if it wasn't for a guy from their team making a three pointer at the buzzer. Basically, with that game I put myself in a position in my coach's head that I had what players call a "Green Light". This means I could take any shot or do anything on the court that I wanted and wouldn't get in trouble for it. So, I used that to my advantage and played some of my best ball since my DeMatha days. The swagger was back and that was because of the hard work I put in after practice.

When it came time for my contract to end I knew that they wouldn't want me to leave, but I was hoping to go somewhere else. I told my agent that because I was playing well, I knew other teams in different countries were taking notice. It was around the time of the year where coaches were looking to make changes, so I wanted to try and make a move. My agents felt that staying could be the best move I could make and that the team would increase my salary.

I was trying to use my stats to get as much money as possible, but I loved the position I was in. I was able to play my game and have fun. That was until I got hurt in a Euro Challenge game in Latvia, which put me on IR (Injured Reserve) for a few weeks. I had already signed for the rest of the season so the team couldn't release me, but made it clear that they wanted me back on the court as soon as possible.

During the time I was on IR, I was enjoying myself off the court a little too much. I was partying and drinking. The city was small and people knew whatever the players were doing. The management pulled me aside and let me know that they did not like what I was doing. I was on IR and should have just been focused on getting back on the court and that's it. I lost focus and started going backwards. It was time for me to get back on the court.

When I did finally get back on the court, I lost some of my swag and confidence. I was training hard and working out after practice, but I didn't have the same relationship with my coach that I had when I was hot. He had heard what I was doing off the court and that only made things worse. There was a strain in our relationship and now we were both in a place where we were frustrated with each other.

I was getting pulled out of the game for little mistakes. My coach felt as though I wasn't the same guy I was when he first arrived. I didn't have that "green light" anymore to play my game. I got to a place where I was miserable being there and was not having fun playing the game I loved.

It was tough and I really tried to stick it out, but the separation from my family didn't help. Although they had been able to come for a month to visit around the holidays, we had been separated for over two months. My wife was struggling with handling the kids alone. On top of that, I was not happy where I was, so I made the decision to forfeit the salary raise and just leave the team and go back home to help my wife.

I figured that I had been playing well enough that another team would soon pick me up. It hurt though that my minutes dropped so much in the last few games that my scoring average went from about 14 points a game to seven. I knew that would have an affect on my next job and the money I would be offered. Also, I had left a team early AGAIN which just fed the reputation I had for not being reliable.

At the time, I felt that going home was the best thing for me. Looking back on it now, I should have just sucked it up and kept on pushing through the remaining two months. I left the team in February and didn't get another job until September. That's seven months without being on a team or collecting an income. That seven-month period was the toughest I have experienced in my professional career.

I have learned a lot during my professional career thus far. I know that nothing is guaranteed in this profession, sometimes not even your salary. And just because you have a job one year, there is no guarantee you will have one the following year. I had to learn the hard way to be careful with my money. My rule now is to spend it like I will not have a job the following year.

I have also finally learned that just because a job with a certain team in a certain league does not seem like a good situation, you have to keep fighting to stay positive no matter what. Once people think you cannot keep your commitments, that reputation can follow you the rest of your career. There are going to be some crazy situations. Just try to handle them the best way possible and think carefully before you decide to leave. Ask yourself if you really can't deal with the situation or is leaving just the easy way out. Going forward, Vanessa and I have made a decision as a family, that despite the challenges that face us with each new team, that we will stick it out for the duration of the season.

TRUST ME, there are ALWAYS going to be obstacles in your life, and that's certainly true of your professional career. That's just life. The question is: are you going to fight through the hard times or try to avoid them? There is an old motivational saying that "Tough times don't build character, they reveal it." I think this is true but I also believe that character is something that can develop by how you deal with and perceive those tough times.

Tough times reveal your character. Will you run or will you fight through them? If you fight through the tough times, then you build your character even more. It's all how you overcome those obstacles that will show your true character. That is what is most important. Character is something that, with the Grace of God, is developed and matured over time. You have to recognize it and want to aspire to it.

FOULS AND FREE THROWS

Develop a Reputation for Class and Character!

Parents: Good decision-making and good character are learned at a very young age. Look for opportunities to teach your child life lessons that will help them make good decisions in adulthood. At the same time, realize that your children will sometimes act in a way that is opposite of what you taught them. That's part of growing up, so just be there for them to help them get back on track. My mom told us over and over again, "A good name is better than great riches." Although I didn't like the reputation I was gaining for leaving teams early, I have always tried to be humble and kind to everyone within the organizations who hired me.

Players: I have never been a coach, so I can only talk about coaching from a player's perspective. However, I did play for the legendary Morgan Wootten who said, "Class gets you to the top and character keeps you at the top." Sometimes, like with Joe Paterno, it takes a while for bad decisions to catch up to you. He spent a lifetime developing Penn State football into a top program. What brought him down was actually years of not reporting wrong doing by one of his coaches. In my case, bad decisions seem to have both immediate and long-term consequences.

Great players who also have great character on and off the court are LOVED by fans and coaches. People are much more forgiving and patient with a player who is in a slump when that player has shown both class and character. Make no mistake, if you don't have talent, class and character won't get you very far as a player, but not having those qualities will always cause you problems.

The people are watching and always trying to put labels on you. When the labels are good, we like them, but you can't always control how you are labeled. All you can do is try your best to develop a reputation for being a good person. I consider myself a pretty classy guy, but I have not always protected my character and reputation and now I am forced to live with labels that don't reflect who I really am.

Be classy and protect your character!!!

9

More than Just a Baller

Becoming a Man

I started this book with the low point of my life when I was arrested and charged with assault and a sex offense. I said that in order for you to understand how I got to the lowest point in my life, you will need to know how I got to the highest point of my basketball life. Becoming a McDonald's All-American and being recruited by the NCAA National Champions are a lot for which to be grateful, but they were less than my highest hopes and dreams.

The high point of my basketball life may have come when I was just a senior in high school, but I look back now and don't believe it was. Honestly, I think the high point for my basketball career is yet to come.

For many players reading this book, your sport is your life. That's how it was for me; I defined myself by how I was ballin'. I love the game and I know how it feels to conquer and I know how it feels to lose.

If I was playing well and people were saying good things about me, I was happy, if I was not playing well or people were being unfair in their criticism, then I was unhappy. I still struggle with that because everyone wants to be liked and admired.

Basketball, just like any sport, can be more than just a game. We develop life long friendships, develop our skills, and learn some pretty hard life lessons through sports. That is why it is important to enjoy your journey as an athlete and not let the opinions of other people be the way you decide if you are happy or not. You've read my story, you know that I let the fans and the sports writers and anyone else who had a negative thing to say about me live in my head. Don't do that! Don't play the game, or live your life, worried about what everyone thinks.

Figure out who loves you because of who you are and take what they tell you seriously. My mom, my dad and brothers, and the elders at my church cared about me as a person. Coaches are amazing. There might be a few coaches you meet along the way that are in it for selfish reasons, but my experience has been that my coaches really cared about me as a person.

You can't let the sports writer who thinks you don't deserve your accolades and the fan in the stands eating his hot dog and yelling, "Hey, Garrison, you suck," be allowed to determine how you feel about yourself. TRUST ME, even getting to the NBA would not equal the way it makes me feel to be a good husband and father and helping people, especially helping young players.

TJ, Vanessa, Jonas, and Travis

The subtitle of this book is "An Athlete's Battle." Life is a battle. The first rule in this battle is don't quit. The second rule is to work on your weaknesses. Remember, your biggest and most powerful enemies are the negative voices in your head and they will attack your weaknesses and draw your attention to your failures. Some of those voices come from other people and we allow them space inside our heads. Then, just as you're about to make that important shot, you hear those voices tell you, "Don't' do it! You will miss and get booed or benched." Some of the voices are just our own self-doubts because as human beings we tend to worry that we aren't good enough or don't deserve to have success.

I have used the words "TRUST ME" a lot in this book. Now I want you to TRUST YOURSELF! Even though I have lost a lot of battles, I have won a lot too, and I intend to win the war. I may not have achieved my dreams when I thought I would, but that doesn't mean they will never happen. I will continue to work to make my dreams come true. Regardless of what anyone else thinks or says, my dream is my dream and no one can discourage me from trying to make it a reality.

Don't get me wrong, I understand that dreams don't come true just because we work hard and don't give up. It may never happen, but when it's all said and done, I want to make sure that I can look back and say I gave it my all. I'm still doing what I love to do. I get to travel the world playing basketball and provide for my family, so no matter what happens, I am really blessed and grateful for what the game of basketball has done for me.

My message to you is this—your dream is your dream. Don't listen to the negative voices, to the sports writers and bloggers, or even the fans in the stands. Don't even listen when they tell you that you are going to the pros. That's a trap that will make you think you can just cruise and make it to the top. Don't get caught up in it. Whatever you did to get to the point where people say you "can't miss," keep doing it! Do not slack off or get distracted. I spent too many years worrying about what other people thought of me. I still play my best basketball when I am just being Travis Garrison and not the player or person other people want me to be.

So what's up for me now? Well, I'm not even 30 years old yet so I have a lot of living to do and I still love the game. One thing I have decided to do is to re-focus myself fully on my game. That's something I haven't done since I was in high school. I have dedicated myself fully to the game; I am not hanging out, drinking, or doing anything else that does not make me a better player. I'm on a strict diet to try to get my body in the best shape possible. I'm in a different time in my life and I don't want to look back five years from now and have any regrets. I'm trying to avoid all negative thinking. Plus Vanessa and I are expecting a baby girl, so I'm trying to provide a bright future for my family.

I want to play at least seven more good seasons and I know I must be in the best shape of my life to do so. I have to have one mind and really be focused. I want to maximize my game the best I possibly can and give my talent the best chance to flourish. That takes discipline, making good decisions and not getting distracted by unnecessary things. I know what it takes, I have done it before and I still have the fire inside.

It's not too late for me to reach my dreams and the real veterans I have played with professionally tell me that I'm still young. I know that the window is closing a little more each year, so I'm trying to take maximum advantage of the time that I have left in my career. That doesn't mean that I won't be just as dedicated to being a good husband and father. In fact, being as successful as possible in my chosen career IS part of being a good man and providing for my family. The best part is that I have a wife who is totally supportive of my goals.

In addition, I am in the process of completing my college degree. As I said earlier, education is something that no one can ever take from you. Although I didn't take it as seriously as I should when I was younger, I know that completing my degree will open a lot more doors for me when I retire from basketball. I also want my children to know that their father has a degree and realize its importance.

When the time comes, I will step aside from playing the game, but I hope to have a career after playing that still involves basketball and helping young players learn the game and to become good people. That is why I wrote this book. I want to lay the foundation for the next phase of my life. I am still spending a lot of time overseas playing ball, but when I am home, I am available to speak at camps, banquets and other events. I want to take advantage of every opportunity to share my story and to help others.

Finally, I want to hear your story, too. I want players and parents, especially, to share with me ways that the story and lessons of my life have helped you or your child. If you are going through some of the same things that I have been through or you are the parent of a player who is, TRUST ME, writing about it helps, so write to me and I will respond.

I can be contacted me by email, on my Facebook page, or on Twitter. I am grateful and honored that you have taken the time to read my book. I look forward to hearing from you.

Travis Garrison

tgneversatisfied@gmail.com

www.facebook.com/ tgneversatisfied

Twitter: @Garrisonhoops

The Million Dollar Question

There is one question that I get asked more than any other. I call it the million dollar question. I get this question the majority of the time from people I know but often I hear it from those I don't know. The million dollar question is, "Travis, knowing the way things worked out, if you could do it ALL over again, would you have chosen the University of Maryland?" And I smile and say, "Well, a good question would be to ask Coach Williams, "Coach, knowing the way things worked out, if you could do it ALL over again would you still have given Travis Garrison a scholarship?"

I don't know what Gary's answer would be, but before I give my answer to the million dollar question, I need to ask my own question to everyone who has asked me that question. "Would you go back and change the things you have done in your past?" Be careful how you answer, it might ultimately change how things are in your life in unforeseen ways.

Before you answer, think about what it might really mean if you had the power to change your past. Say, hypothetically speaking, that I would have gone to another college to play ball. And let's say that I do what some predicted and after a year or two of playing great ball in college, I got drafted and became a successful NBA player.

Sounds good on the surface, as a matter of fact, it sounds great! But to achieve that fantasy life, I just had to eliminate a lot of the obstacles and challenges that I faced and had to learn to face and overcome like a man at the University of Maryland. Now what happens when I'm in that NBA fantasy life and I am faced with something I have never been through before? What resources would I have to handle my problems? What if I get in a situation that could possibly destroy my career and ruin my life?

It isn't just about changing one decision; I would have to be able to keep using the power to skip over real life problems because that's how I got out of all the things that happened at Maryland. Then what? Can you guarantee that I would be married to my beautiful wife of four years? Would I have these beautiful kids? Would I be half the man I am today in this fantasy world?

I'm not going to lie; I have asked myself the same question. I actually asked my wife the "what if" question and she kind of summed it all up to me like this, "Babe, if things would have gone like they were supposed to, or the way you planned for them to, then we probably would have never met." Wow! And there it is, if things would have gone like I WANTED them to go, I probably wouldn't be with Vanessa nor in a position to help other people learn how not to make the same mistakes I've made.

I probably wouldn't be able to give anybody the courage to keep pushing when things seem rough because I got this slick power to avoid the decisions I made in the past. That's not a power I can give to someone who is in trouble or hurting. So, the answer to what turns out to be a ten cent question is, NO, I would not change ANYTHING. I have NO regrets, but I do have life learning lessons that I have been blessed to share in this book.

Now I have a story to tell and players and parents, and coaches can use my story to help themselves, their children, or their players to overcome any obstacle. I want others to know the good and the bad, the ups and the downs, how the "can't miss" kid missed and how I came through it all to be the man that I am today. I don't want or need the super power to change the past. I want the power within me to fight through the battles to come and to help others do the same thing.

I don't know what answer Gary Williams would give to that question, but I know that I am a better person because of the four years I spent playing for him. I am happy to say that I am now in a position where I am not ashamed of the mistakes I made. I accept full responsibility without blaming anyone else. I am willing to be transparent to people so they can learn from my mistakes and learn from my story.

I also know that I have done some good things in my life. I am not defined by my mistakes or the voices that still want to live in the past, to go back and ask, "What happened?" The great thing is that, however much this story and its lessons might help others, they are still helping me to this day to become a better man. I hope they do the same for you.

Made in the USA
Charleston, SC
02 October 2012